MASONRY

and

ITS SYMBOLS

By Harold Waldwin Percival

ISBN: 978-1-63923-465-3

Printed: July 2022

Cover Art By: Amit Paul

Published and Distributed By:
Lushena Books
607 Country Club Drive, Unit E
Bensenville, IL 60106
www.lushenabks.com

ISBN: 978-1-63923-465-3

MASONRY

and

ITS SYMBOLS

In the Light of
Thinking and Destiny

by

Harold W. Percival

DEDICATION

Dedicated with Love to the Conscious Self in every Mason
with the hope that this book will help all Masons to get more
Light through their symbols.

TABLE OF CONTENTS

FOREWORD viii

PREFACE ix

SECTION 1   The Brotherhood of Freemasons. Compass.
Membership. Age. Temples. Intelligences behind Masonry.
Purpose and plan. Masonry and religions. The essential
and the temporary teachings. The fundamental principles
of the three degrees. Offshoots. Great truths locked up
in trivial forms. The secret language. Passive and active
thinking. Lines on the breath-form. Discipline of desires
and of mental operations. The ancient landmarks. Masons
should see the importance of their Order.................1

SECTION 2   Meaning of the preliminaries. A free man.
Recommendation. Preparations in the heart and for
initiation. The divestment. The hoodwink. The fourfold
cable-tow. The candidate is the conscious self in the
body. Travels. The sharp instrument. Instructions. The
pledge. The three great lights and the lesser lights. What
the candidate learns about these symbols. Signs, grips
and words. The symbol of the lambskin. The scene of
poverty. The Mason as an upright man. His working
tools. Declaration of the Apprentice. The signs and their
meanings. The Word. The four virtues. The six jewels.
The Ground Floor of King Solomon's Temple. Purpose of
the symbols and ceremonies 6

SECTION 3   The degree of Fellow Craft. How the candidate
is received and the meaning of it. Being brought to light.
What he receives. The tools of a Fellow Craft. Their
meaning. The two Columns. Building the bridge from
Boaz to Jachin. The three, five and seven steps. The
Middle Chamber. Meaning of the steps. The wages and
the jewels. Meaning of the letter G. The point and the
circle. The four and the three degrees. The twelve points
on the circle. The Zodiacal signs. Expression of universal
truths. Geometry. The achievements of the Fellow Craft.
The Thinker. The Master Mason. Preparation. Reception.
Being brought to light. The pass, the grip, the apron and
the tools of a Master Mason..........................13

SECTION 4   Life, death and resurrection of Hiram Abiff.
The great lesson of Masonry. What Hiram symbolizes.
The two triangles. The designs on the trestle-board. The
South gate. The workmen. Hiram is restrained from
going out. He is slain at the East gate. The immortal
body. Jubela, Jubelo, Jubelum. Meanings of these three
symbols. The three assaults. The Masonic drama. The
fifteen workmen. The Great Twelve. The pairs of triangles
forming six-pointed stars. Hiram as the power that
makes the round. The finding of the three ruffians. The
three burials of Hiram. The raising by King Solomon.
The monument at the place of burial. Raising of the
candidate. The three columns. The forty-seventh problem
of Euclid 20

SECTION 5   Meaning of the lodge as a room and as the
brothers. The officers, their stations and duties. The
three degrees as the foundation of Masonry. The work. A
Mason's own lodge. 28

SECTION 6   The cable-tow. The Royal Arch. The candidate
as the keystone. Realization of the great Masonic symbol.
The fifth degree. The fourth degree. The keystone with
the mark of Hiram. The sixth degree. Another aspect
of the keystone symbol. The union of Boaz and Jachin.
The Glory of the Lord fills the Lord's house. The seventh
degree. The Tabernacle. The Master's jewels and the Ark
of the Covenant. The Name and the Word 31

SECTION 7   Summary of the teachings of Masonry. They
center around "Light." The symbols, acts and words of
the ritual. Ritualists and their workings. The permanent
forms of Masonry and twisted teachings. Scriptural
passages. Geometrical symbols. Their value. Masonry has
in trust certain geometrical symbols which, coordinated in
a system for the Masonic work, are thus preserved 37

SYMBOLS AND ILLUSTRATIONS. 43

DEFINITIONS AND EXPLANATIONS 49

INDEX. 71

FOREWORD

Greetings to all members of Ancient Free and Accepted Masonry throughout the world. Every Mason understands that his advancement through degrees in Masonry is a journey in search of "more Light" or a quest for knowledge and truth. Masonic degrees, their meaning and ritual of conferment, are deeply steeped in symbolism which transcends all language barriers; therefore the universal appeal of Masonry for thousands of years. Masons also know that rituals and ceremonial badges are meaningless unless each Brother lives according to the obligations he has so solemnly assumed. By understanding the meaning of the symbols Masons, and non-Masons alike, will come to see these symbols as guideposts on our road of life as we seek to find our way back to The Realm of Permanence* whence we came.

Masonry and Its Symbols, more than any other book known to the Fraternity, provides a link between the esoteric meanings of Ancient Masonry and the more familiar exoteric meanings of today. It will enhance every Mason's likelihood of finding "more Light."

I have been privileged to be a member of the Fraternity for 37 years and a student of this book for 23 of those years. To my Brothers, I sincerely recommend *Masonry and Its Symbols* as priority reading to augment your complete understanding of Masonry.

C. F. Cope, Master Mason
September, 1983

---

* *The Realm of Permanence is defined and clarified in* Thinking and Destiny. *It can also be found in the Definitions section of this book.—Ed.*

PREFACE

The symbols and rituals of Freemasonry, the fraternal order of Masonry, are integral to greater understanding of ourselves, the universe, and beyond; however, they can often seem inscrutable, perhaps even to some Masons. *Masonry and Its Symbols* illuminates the meaning, character and truth of these geometrical forms. Once we perceive the inherent significance of these symbols we also have the opportunity to comprehend our ultimate mission in life. That mission is that each human, in some life, must regenerate his or her human imperfect body, thereby rebuilding a perfectly balanced, sexless, immortal physical body. This is referred to in Masonry as the "second temple" that will be greater than the first.

Mr. Percival offers an in depth view of one of the strongest tenants of Masonry, the rebuilding of King Solomon's temple. This is not to be understood as an edifice made of mortar or metal, but "the temple not made with hands." According to the author, Freemasonry trains the human so that the candidate may eventually reconstruct the mortal body into a deathless spiritual temple "eternal in the heavens."

Rebuilding our mortal body is the destiny of the human, our ultimate path, although it may seem a daunting one. But with the realization of what we truly are and how we came to this earthly sphere, we develop the moral fortitude in our daily lives to learn "what to do and what not to do" in each situation we encounter. This is important because our response to those life events determines our path in being conscious in ever higher degrees, which is fundamental to the regeneration process itself.

Should one wish to further investigate this subject matter, *Thinking and Destiny* can serve as a guidebook. First published in 1946 and now in its fourteenth printing, it is also available to read on our website. Within this comprehensive and expansive book one can find information about the entirety of the universe and mankind, including the long-forgotten past of the present human.

The author originally intended that *Masonry and Its Symbols* be included as a chapter in *Thinking and Destiny*. He later decided to delete that chapter from the manuscript and publish it under separate cover. Because some of the terms advanced in *Thinking and Destiny* would be helpful to the reader, these are now referenced in a "Definitions" section of this book. For ease of reference, the symbols alluded to by the author in his "Legend to Symbols" have also been included.

The abundance and depth of material presented in *Thinking and Destiny* should nourish any person's quest for knowledge of our true origin and purpose in life. With this realization, *Masonry and Its Symbols* will not only become more comprehensible, but one's life may well be set on a new course.

The Word Foundation
November, 2014

SECTION 1

The Brotherhood of Freemasons. Compass. Membership. Age. Temples. Intelligences behind Masonry. Purpose and plan. Masonry and religions. The essential and the temporary teachings. The fundamental principles of the three degrees. Offshoots. Great truths locked up in trivial forms. The secret language. Passive and active thinking. Lines on the breath-form. Discipline of desires and of mental operations. The ancient landmarks. Masons should see the importance of their Order.

The Brotherhood of Freemasons is the largest of the bodies in the world which are outposts to prepare possible candidates for an inward life. They are men drawn from all ranks and races for whose character and intelligence a Master Mason has at one time vouched. Masonry is for Humanity, the conscious self in every human body, not for any special race, religion or clique.

The Order existed under one name or another as a compact, well-organized body long before the building of the oldest pyramid. It is older than any religion known today. It is the extraordinary thing among organizations in the world. This organization and the system of its teachings, with the tools, landmarks, emblems and symbols, have always been substantially the same. It goes back to the age when bodies became male or female. The temple has always been a symbol of a rebuilt human body. Some of the legendary masonic temples, whose place is now taken by that of Solomon, were circles, ovals, squares and oblongs of stones. Sometimes the stones were connected at the top by slabs, later by two pieces of stone pitted against each other in triangular form, and then by semicircular arches. Sometimes the temples were enclosed by walls; these temples were open at the top, and the vault of heaven was the roof. So symbolic temples were built for the worship of the Lord, until the last that figures in the Masonic ritual is called Solomon's Temple.

Intelligences in the earth sphere are behind Masonry, though the lodges are not aware of this in the present age. The spirit that runs through the system of the masonic teachings connects these Intelligences with every Mason, from the greatest to the least, who practices them.

The purpose of Masonry is to train a human being so that he will reconstruct, through the body of change and death which he now has, a perfect physical body which shall not be subject to death. The plan is to build this deathless body, called by modern Masons Solomon's Temple, out of material in the physical body, which is called the ruins of Solomon's Temple. The plan is to build a temple not made with hands, eternal in the heavens, which is the cryptic name for the deathless physical vesture. The Masons say that in the building of Solomon's Temple there was not heard the sound of an axe, hammer or any tool of iron; nor will any sound be heard in the rebuilding of the temple. A Masonic prayer is: "And since sin has destroyed within us the first temple of purity and innocence, may thy heavenly grace guide and assist us in rebuilding a second temple of reformation, and may the glory of this latter house be greater than the glory of the former."

There are no better and no more advanced teachings available to human beings, than those of Masonry. The symbols used in the Craft are chiefly tools of a mason and instruments of an architect. The symbols have been substantially the same from immemorial times; though their shape and interpretation have changed, and though the rituals and lectures about them changed with the prevailing cyclic religion of the age. The doctrines of all religions are so made that they can be used for masonic teachings. In modern western Masonry, that

2

is, what the Masons call Ancient Masonry, Masonry is given in forms of the Hebrew religion, with some additions from the New Testament. The teachings are not Hebrew. But Masonry uses parts of Hebrew traditions to clothe and present its own teachings, because the Hebrew traditions are familiar and acceptable as parts of the Bible. The masonic teachings might be presented in Egyptian or pre-Egyptian Greek clothes, if the people were familiar with them. The Hebrew traditions are colorful and impressive. Besides, the physical body in which the reconstruction has to go on is the divided name of Jah-veh or Jah-hovah. Yet the rituals are sometimes easily shaped to exemplify Christianity, by making Christ the Supreme Grand Master, and the Great Architect of the Universe can be interpreted as a Christian God. But Masonry is not Christian any more than it is Jewish. The temporary interpretations according to age and place and religion are looked upon by the common run of Masons as absolute and as the truth.

Often the symbology is obscured by adornments, additions, changes and omissions. Sometimes whole Orders are instituted in these ways and specialize a particular religious, warlike, or social feature. They disappear again, while the symbols and the teachings of which they are a part, remain.

The principles of Masonry are represented in the first three degrees, those of Entered Apprentice, Fellow Craft, and Master Mason, and in the development of those degrees in the Holy Royal Arch. The principles there represented are fundamental, whether found in the York rite, the Scottish rite, or in any other masonic rite. Some rites have degrees which are merely local, personal, social and inviting. There are many side rites, side issues, side degrees, which gifted ritualists have brought into existence, but the principles of Masonry are few and survive the ages and their styles.

Masonry is the trunk or physical connection from which different Orders are formed from time to time. Rosicrucianism in the Middle Ages and other movements of a later date were offshoots put out through members of the Masonic Order, to meet a need of the times without entangling Masonry itself.

In many of the forms of the masonic work that seem trivial and childish are locked up great truths. The truths have to be presented in some symbol or by some work, because human beings need forms in which to see truths. They call truths platitudes, yet cannot see them. When truths are put into forms which are parts of physical life, an apt and striking application of such truths impresses itself upon those who see and feel the application and holds their interest.

It is possible to arrange, and Masonry does arrange, information about fundamental truths about the conscious self and its relation to nature in a systematic way, though in simple forms. By constant repetition of these forms their application to life in general becomes evident. The words used in connection with these forms become a secret language whether the forms be symbols, jewels, tools, badges, emblems, degrees, steps, signs, grips, words, ceremonies, points, lines, angles, surfaces, or simple stories. A common language is a bond of brotherhood, and a secret language which is not bestowed by birth, as is the language of one's country, but by common choice and service, is one of the strongest ties that hold men together. Also by going through these forms over and over they are engraved by sight and sound upon the breath-form and cause passive thinking along the engraved lines. Later active thinking results along the same lines, and with it comes the Light by which the particular truth concealed in the form is seen. After death the lines, made on the breath-form by masonic thinking and masonic thoughts, play an important part in shaping

4

destiny. In the next life on earth a Mason comes under the masonic influences, though he be born under and be claimed by the spirit of a race or of a religion.

The forms of the masonic work are designed to further a discipline of feelings and desires and three minds. The desires are disciplined by thinking which sets bounds to them, and the three minds themselves are disciplined by thinking according to the forms. Only a few subjects are presented in the many masonic forms. These subjects reappear and force themselves upon the attention of a Mason. The forms after a while become suggestive of the subjects for which they stand and so engage mental activity. The discipline results from the regular exercise of the mental activity along the aspects of an inner life which the forms are designed to symbolize.

The forms preserve the secret teachings and in that respect are of inestimable value. The forms are the ancient landmarks of the Order, entrusted to the care of Masons which they are to preserve carefully and are never to suffer to be infringed.

Such are some of the purposes which the masonic play serves. Though what Masons see and hear and say and do has a deep esoteric meaning, they are not affected by that, but delight in the play, the speeches and the social features. Masons seldom, if ever, see the importance of their Order and of its purposes. When they see the inner meanings of their work and begin to live according to their teachings, they will become better men, have a broader and deeper understanding of life, and make the Order of Freemasons a living power for good in the world.

SECTION 2

Meaning of the preliminaries. A free man. Recommendation.
Preparations in the heart and for initiation. The divestment.
The hoodwink. The fourfold cable-tow. The candidate is the
conscious self in the body. Travels. The sharp instrument.
Instructions. The pledge. The three great lights and the
lesser lights. What the candidate learns about these symbols.
Signs, grips and words. The symbol of the lambskin. The
scene of poverty. The Mason as an upright man. His
working tools. Declaration of the Apprentice. The signs and
their meanings. The Word. The four virtues. The six jewels.
The Ground Floor of King Solomon's Temple. Purpose of the
symbols and ceremonies.

Before one can become a Freemason he must be a free man. A slave cannot be a Mason. In a wider sense he must not be a slave to lust and avarice. He must be sufficiently free to choose of his own free will and accord, that is, not be bound down by base desires or blind to the facts of life. To become a Freemason the candidate must be recommended as to character. He must be in some measure a searcher into the mysteries of life. He must desire more light and be in search of it.

The first preparation is to be made in his heart. He appoints himself to be a Mason and prepares himself by having an honest, clean heart. When a Mason meets with such a man, he will, believing that the other will be a good member, bring the conversation on subjects which will lead the candidate to express his desire to seek admission into a lodge. After the application is made, investigated and recommended, the candidate will be prepared for admission. After he is admitted there is a further preparation for initiation in the anteroom of the lodge.

He is there divested of his clothing. That ceremony stands for the removal of the things that hold him to the outer world, such as possessions and indications of station and rank. It means that he is separated from the past, so

6

that he can enter on a new course. When he is stripped it will appear that he is a man, not a woman. A hoodwink or blind is put over his eyes, so that he feels he is in darkness, without light, and cannot find his way. Then the thing he most desires is light.

A rope, a cable-tow—it should be a rope of four strands—is put around him. It symbolizes the bond by which all Apprentices, Craftsmen and Masons have been entered, initiated, passed and raised into the light of Masonry. The cable-tow stands for the umbilical cord by which all bodies are prepared for birth. It stands for the senses of sight, hearing, taste and smell by which the candidate (the conscious self in the body) is held after birth, which bind him to nature and lead him in darkness. It stands for Masonry which brings him out of the physical world of darkness into the Light. The cable-tow stands for the tie that binds, into a brotherhood of whatever kind. The cable-tow also is the line on the breath-form that binds one to Masonry, to destiny, to rebirth and re-existence.

He begins his work and his travels naked, in darkness, tied to humanity and its common failings. He feels the touch of a sharp instrument; his flesh is pricked to remind him of the torture to which it may put him, and that he must nevertheless persevere with the work to which he will dedicate himself. He is instructed in the conduct of life, always with his work as the end in view. He calls on God, his Triune Self, to witness his obligation and gives his pledge to preserve himself inviolate to the work. To continue his work he needs more light, and he declares that that which he most desires is light. The symbolical hoodwink or blind is removed and he is brought to light. At birth into the world the cord is severed. Likewise when the Apprentice is brought to the light, which is the new tie, the cable-tow is removed. Then he is told that the Bible, the square and the compass, on which he has taken his obligation and to which he has dedicated himself, represent the three great Lights. The three lighted candles, he is told, represent the three lesser lights: the sun, the moon and the Master of the Lodge.

If the Apprentice keeps his obligation, and does the work, he learns, by these symbols, as he advances, that he receives the Word of God, the Light of lights, through his Knower. He learns that as the compass describes a line equally distant throughout from the point around which it is drawn, so the mind, according to its light, keeps the passions and desires in bounds which are measured by reason and are of equal distance from the rightness, the center. He learns that as the square is used to draw and prove all straight lines, to make two lines at right angles to one another and to unite horizontals with perpendiculars, so by himself as the Doer all feelings and desires are made straight, are put in the right relation to each other and are united with each other.

He will learn, after he is raised, that the three great Lights are verily symbols of the three parts of his Triune Self; that the Bible, or sacred writings, which is symbolic of his Knower, which is Gnosis, is the source through which he must get Light; and that instead of the points of the compass being under the square they must be over it for him to get that Light, that is to say, Rightness, the right point, and Reason, the left point, of the compass, must set bounds to feeling, the right line, and to desire, the left line of the square.

He will learn that there are connected with him, at present, only two of the great lights, the Bible and the Compass; that the points of the square are above the compass; that is to say, his feeling and desire are not controlled by his Rightness and Reason, and that the third Light, the square, is dark, that is, the Light does not reach his feeling-and-desire. The third Light was shut out at the destruction of the first temple; it is potential only and will not be an actual Light until the temple is rebuilt.

The three lesser lights, the sun, the moon and the Master of the Lodge symbolize the body, feeling-and-desire, and their minds. The lodge is the human body. The light for the body, that is nature, is the sun. The moon reflects sunlight. The moon is feeling, on which are reflected the objects of nature by the body, which is personalized nature and is the servant of outside nature. The third light is the Master or desire, and he ought to endeavor to rule

8

and govern his lodge, that is, the body. The body-mind should be used to govern the body and its four senses; the feeling-mind should govern itself, and the desire-mind as the Master should govern itself in the coordination of the feelings and the control of the body.

The Apprentice, as he advances, receives the signs, grips and words, by which he can prove himself or another, in the light or in the dark, and among those not Masons, according to the degree of his light in Masonry. He learns to walk as a Mason should, on the square.

He receives a lambskin, or white apron, a symbol of his physical body. He who wears the lambskin as a badge of a Mason is thereby continually reminded of that purity of life and conduct which is necessary. The apron clothes the pelvic region and is a symbol that that should be kept clean. It refers to sex and food. As he grows in knowledge he should preserve the body not in innocence, but in purity. When he is able to wear the apron as a Master Mason should, the flap which may be an equilateral or a right-angled triangle, hangs over the square with the corners down. The apron as a square symbolizes the four elements of nature working in the fourfold body through its four systems and the four senses. The triangular flap stands for the three parts of the Triune Self, and the three minds as substitutes for the Triune Self. They are above the body or not entirely in the body in the case of the Apprentice, and within the body or fully embodied in the case of the Master.

When asked to contribute to a worthy cause the Apprentice finds he is penniless, unable to do so, naked and an object of charity. This is a reminder to aid those whom he finds in life and who are in need of help. The scene should make him feel that he is nothing more or less than what he is as a man; that he should be judged by what he is and not be valued in terms of dress, possessions, a title, or money.

He is then allowed to reclothe himself; he puts on his apron and is taken before the Master of the Lodge who directs him to stand at his right hand and tells him that he is now an upright man, a Mason, and charges him ever to walk and act as such. As a Mason, he must have working tools. He is given the working tools of an Apprentice which are the twenty-four inch gauge and common gavel.

The gauge is the symbol of masculinity. It has to do not only with the hours but with the span of life. The gauge is the rule of life and the rule of right. The first third is for the Apprentice when he should, as the masonic ritual has it, remember his Creator in the days of his youth. This is the service of God, by not wasting the creative power. Thereby he fits himself to follow his masonic work in the second degree as a Fellow Craft. He then is rebuilding his body, the temple not made with hands. The last third is for the Master Mason who is refreshed by the conserved power and is a master builder.

The gavel is said to be an instrument which operative masons use to break off the superfluous corners of rough stones to fit them for the builder's use, but with the speculative Mason the gavel stands for the force of desire which should be used with the gauge, or rule of right, to remove inherited inclinations and vices, so that each life of the Mason may be shaped into and become a living stone, a perfect ashler, in the final temple of the Triune Self. His first life, that in which he becomes an Apprentice, is said to be a corner stone, from which a super-structure of an immortal physical body is expected to rise.

The Apprentice declares that he has come into Masonry to learn to subdue his passions and improve himself in Masonry. It is the profession of his purpose. He is asked how he will know himself to be or how he may be known to be a Mason, and he declares that he will do it by certain signs, a token, a word and the perfect points of his entrance.

The signs, he says, are right angles, horizontals and perpendiculars, which must be parallel. These signs mean more than how he shall step or hold his hands or pose his body.

The right angles mean the squaring of his feeling (one line) with his desire (the other line) in all actions.

The horizontals mean the equal balancing of his feeling and of his desire.

The perpendiculars mean that his feeling and desire are raised to uprightness from lowness.

The token is a grip. It means that he must hold his feeling and his desire with a firm grip, and it also means that feeling and desire should grip each other in the same degree and prove each other.

A word is the one used in the Apprentice degree, and is a symbol. Lines make letters, and letters a word. Four letters are needed to make The Word. The Apprentice can supply only one letter, that letter is A and is made of two lines, feeling and desire. The Word is found by the Royal Arch Mason.

The perfect points of the Apprentice's entrance are four. They are the four cardinal virtues: temperance is habitual self-restraint or control of one's passionate impulses and appetites; fortitude means constant courage, patience and endurance without fear of danger; prudence means skill in right thinking and in the performance of right action; and justice is knowledge of the rights of oneself and others, and in thinking and acting in accordance with that knowledge.

The candidate learns about the jewels. There are six jewels, three movable, which are the rough ashler, the perfect ashler, and the trestle-board. The rough ashler is the symbol of the present, imperfect physical body; the perfect ashler is the symbol of the physical body after it has been perfected, and the trestle-board the symbol of the breath-form, on which the designs of the building are drawn. These three jewels are called movable because they perish after each life or are carried from life to life. The immovable jewels are the square, the level and the plumb. The square symbolizes desire, the level feeling and the plumb the pattern of the perfect body which is on the breath-form. These three are called immovable, because they are of the Triune Self and do not die.

The First Degree, that of Entered Apprentice, relates to the initiation of himself as Doer of feeling-and-desire. This is done on the Ground Floor of Solomon's Temple, that is, in the pelvic region. The Apprentice first prepares himself in his heart, then he is prepared for initiation by being separated from his past. After he has traveled, has been brought to light, has received some information about the three greater Lights by means of the three lesser lights, has received his white apron, is clothed again and has seen the blazing star, he is given the working tools of an Entered Apprentice and then makes certain declarations. All of the symbols and ceremonies are intended to impress upon him what to do with his desires and the use of his desire-mind, feeling-mind, and body-mind in his conduct towards himself, his brothers, and his God.

SECTION 3

*The degree of Fellow Craft. How the candidate is received and
the meaning of it. Being brought to light. What he receives.
The tools of a Fellow Craft. Their meaning. The two Columns.
Building the bridge from Boaz to Jachin. The three, five and
seven steps. The Middle Chamber. Meaning of the steps. The
wages and the jewels. Meaning of the letter G. The point and
the circle. The four and the three degrees. The twelve points
on the circle. The Zodiacal signs. Expression of universal
truths. Geometry. The achievements of the Fellow Craft. The
Thinker. The Master Mason. Preparation. Reception. Being
brought to light. The pass, the grip, the apron and the tools
of a Master Mason.*

The second degree, that of Fellow Craft, is not an
initiation of the Thinker, but is the passing of the
conscious Doer from the darkness and ignorance of
feeling-and-desire to the light of Rightness-and-Reason.
He is received into this degree on the angle of the square,
symbolic of the fact that he has made his feeling-and-desire
right and square, at right angles with each other, that
he has united them, and that they will be used so in all
his actions. He asks for more light and is shown how to
step towards that Light. He receives more Light. In being
brought to Light in this degree, he perceives one point of
the compass above the square, symbolic of the fact that
he receives Light through the Rightness of his Thinker
and that he will be guided in his actions from that point,
that Light. He receives the pass, the grip and the word
of a Fellow Craft. The pass is symbolical of the transfer
or passage from the first to the second degree. The grip
stands for the power of Rightness over feeling-and-desire.
The word is still not the Word, but is only two letters,
namely the A with a U or an O.

He is given the working tools of a Fellow Craft
which are the plumb, the square and the level. The plumb
stands for uprightness in thinking, the level for equality in
thinking, and the square for the union of the plumb and the

13

level. This means that the signs which were only lines in the Apprentice degree have now in the Fellow Craft degree become tools; the perpendiculars and horizontals, which were lines, have become the plumb and the level, and the right angles have become the square. Desire and feeling are now upright and level, united, that is, in agreement with and in right relation to each other, and act from the point of their union which is at Rightness. The angle of the square stands for the point of union. The square is used in thinking, whether by the plumb or on the level, in all that concerns the earth, that is, the physical body of oneself or of another.

He is shown two brazen columns, said to have been at the entrance of Solomon's Temple. Boaz, the left column, symbolizes the sympathetic or nature column, which will be in front of the body, and Jachin, the right one, is the spinal column, the column of the Triune Self. When the Doer part of the Triune Self first came into its body, that is, its temple, the body was neither male nor female, and the two columns existed and functioned having the united power. After its temple was destroyed, the Doer functioned in a body which was either male or female and had only Jachin, the male column, and had only the power of the male or of the female. Boaz does not exist, except potentially. The Fellow Craft is reminded by seeing the two columns that he has to rebuild Boaz. The stones which the Apprentice has prepared with his rule and gavel are to be further prepared by the Fellow Craft for the Master Mason before Boaz will be re-established. It is significant that the chapiters of both columns show network, lily-work and pomegranates full of seeds. The network is that of interlaced nerves which is built up by purity which preserves the seeds, and which builds the bridge from Boaz to Jachin.

The Fellow Craft sees the three, five and seven steps or stairs as the winding stairs leading to the Middle Chamber of Solomon's Temple. The five steps are symbolic of work in the Fellow Craft degree, while the three steps relate to the Apprentice degree through which he has passed and the work of which he continues.

The three, five and seven steps or stairs are certain centers or organs in the body. The body as a whole is

SECTION 3

King Solomon's Temple (or the ruins of it from which the
temple is to be rebuilt). The entrance or first step is the
prostate, the second step symbolizes the kidneys, the third
the adrenals, the fourth the heart, the fifth the lungs, the
sixth the pituitary body and the seventh the pineal body.
These steps are taken by the use of the minds of Rightness
and of Reason. The body-mind is used by the Apprentice
to control the body, the feeling-mind to control feeling and
the desire-mind to control desire. By controlling feeling
he controls feelings, and by controlling desire, he controls
desires. The candidate is always the Doer part of the
Triune Self, throughout the work of the three degrees. His
taking the five steps of the Fellow Craft means the ability
to reach the minds used by and for Rightness and Reason
of the Thinker of his Triune Self. His taking the seven
steps symbolizes his reaching to the minds which are used
by and for I-ness and selfness.

The white apron or clean body, which is the badge of
a Mason, the rule of right and the gavel of desire are the
three steps; by them the Apprentice prepares stones for
building. The five are the same three together with the
two, the plumb and the level, added. When uprightness
in thinking is united with equality in thinking, the plumb
and the level form the square, the point of union being at
Rightness. With these five the Fellow Craft prepares and
fits the building stones. The building stones are the units
of nature. The seven are a symbol for the seven minds
and seven powers of the minds to develop which the Fellow
Craft is called. Speculative Masonry designates these seven
aspects by the names of the liberal arts and sciences, which
are given as grammar, rhetoric, logic, arithmetic, geometry,
music and astronomy. The great Three, Five and Seven,
though here mentioned, are not brought into the ritual,
except that the three, five and seven are brought into
relation with the development of the Doer of feeling-and-
desire to use its minds.

The ascent through a porch, by a flight of winding
stairs, consisting of three, five and seven steps, to a place
representing the Middle Chamber of King Solomon's Temple,
that is, the lodge working in the Fellow Craft degree, is also
symbolical of various windings of nature to her concealed

15

recesses, that is, certain physiological developments, due to the development of one's minds, by thinking, before he is received and recorded as a Fellow Craft.

The wages and jewels he receives for his work as a Fellow Craft are certain psychic and mental powers, symbolized by corn, wine and oil, and by the attentive ear, instructive tongue and faithful breast.

The attention of the Fellow Craft is directed to a great symbol placed above the head of the Master, the letter G. It is said to stand for God, for Gnosis and for Geometry. But it has not been at all times a Roman G. The G stands in place of that which is universally symbolized by the point in the center of a circle.

The point and the circle are the same, the point is the infinitesimally small circle and the circle is the point fully expressed. The expression is divided into the manifested and the unmanifested. The expression proceeds by points and lines. The unmanifested is present in the manifested and the manifested is in the unmanifested. The purpose of the expression is to make that which becomes manifested, conscious of and to identify itself with the unmanifested which is within it; then the circle is fully expressed and the expression, by degrees, re-becomes the point. The expression is divided into the unmanifested or Substance and the manifested or matter. Matter is again divided into nature-matter and intelligent-matter, according to degrees in which the matter is conscious. These degrees are proved by the square and described by the compass, according to angles, horizontals and perpendiculars. Nature-matter is divided infinitely according to the subdegrees of the four elements, and their combinations and subdivisions, and their hierarchies of beings in the four manifested worlds. Intelligent-matter, that is, the Triune Self, is divided into three degrees, those of Apprentice, Fellow Craft and Master. These are exalted in the Royal Arch, which is in Substance, beyond matter. The unmanifested is always in the manifested on the nature-side as well as on the intelligent-side, but it can be approached and found in the intelligent-side only. It is found by being conscious, which in Masonry is called getting more Light.

SECTION 3

The point and the circle stand for all this and for more. The meaning of the fully expressed circle can be rendered by symbols, twelve in number, which stand for twelve points on the circle. Every being and thing in the manifested worlds and the unmanifested universe has a sharply marked value, nature and place, according to some of these points.

The best symbols to indicate the twelve points of the circle are the Zodiacal signs. Universal truths can be expressed through the Zodiac in a way which ordinary language does not permit and so can be understood, after a fashion, by men. To illustrate, the Universe, as well as a cell, is divided by a line from Cancer to Capricorn into the unmanifested above and the manifested below. Matter is separated by a line from Aries to Libra into nature-matter and intelligent-matter. "Souls" enter by conception at the gate of Cancer of the physical world, and are born at the gate of Libra and pass on at the gate of Capricorn. The square is made by the line from Cancer to Libra and by the line from Libra to Capricorn, and the Master sits in the East, at Capricorn, and rules his lodge on this square, the angle of which is at Libra. The square of the Great Architect is the square from Cancer to Libra to Capricorn of the Universe, over and above the four worlds of Cancer, Leo, Virgo, and Libra. So the signs of the Zodiac, as symbols of the twelve points of the fully expressed circle, speak an accurate language that reaches everything in the Universe. This language is that for which the word Geometry stands. The Fellow Craft is told that this is also symbolized by the letter G.

Geometry is half of the science, the other half is the geometer. Geometry deals with only one of the tools, namely the square, which is used to draw straight lines, horizontals and perpendiculars, and to prove corners. The other tool, the compass, stands for the other half, the Geometer, or the Intelligence, without which there could be no Geometry. The compass draws curved lines between two points and describes a circle which is one continuous line without end, each part of which is equally distant from the center. Within the bounds of the circle, all true building must be erected on the square.

The Apprentice has passed into the Fellow Craft. The Fellow Craft has received more Light and has learned the use of his tools; he understands how to rebuild the two columns and how to ascend the winding stairs by the three, five and seven steps. The symbols and the work in this degree relate to the minds of feeling-and-desire coming under the guidance of the minds of Rightness and Reason of the Thinker of the Triune Self. By the plumb and the level of his thinking the Fellow Craft adjusts feeling-and-desire. He causes all the feelings and desires to be squared on the inner as well as on the outer expressions. He does all this by his thinking.

The degree of Master Mason represents the Apprentice and Fellow Craft raised to the degree of Master. As the Apprentice is the Doer and the Fellow Craft the Thinker, so the Master Mason is the Knower. Going through each degree as an individual symbolizes the development of the Apprentice or Doer passing to the Fellow Craft or relation to the Thinker and being raised to the degree of Master Mason or attaining to relation to the Knower.

The candidate after he is prepared, blindfolded and tied with cable-tow around his waist, enters the lodge. He is received on both points of the compass, pressed against his breast. He takes the three steps to the altar where he kneels for the third time, rests his hands on the Bible, square and compass, and takes the obligation of a Master Mason. He asks for further light in Masonry. He is brought to light by the Master of the lodge, and hoodwink and cable-tow removed. Thus he sees that both points of the compass are above the square. This is a symbol that with one who has reached this degree both aspects of the Thinker are operative above feeling-and-desire because feeling-and-desire have put themselves under the guidance of the Thinker. He receives the pass and grip of a Master Mason and wears his apron as a Master Mason, that is, with the flap and all corners down.

The working tools of a Master are all the implements of Masonry of the three degrees, more especially the trowel. As the gauge and mallet prepared the rough stones, as the plumb, level and square fitted them into position, so the trowel spreads the cement and completes the work of the Apprentice and Fellow Craft.

SECTION 4

*Life, death and resurrection of Hiram Abiff. The great lesson
of Masonry. What Hiram symbolizes. The two triangles. The
designs on the trestle-board. The South gate. The workmen.
Hiram is restrained from going out. He is slain at the East
gate. The immortal body. Jubela, Jubelo, Jubelum. Meanings
of these three symbols. The three assaults. The Masonic drama.
The fifteen workmen. The Great Twelve. The pairs of triangles
forming six-pointed stars. Hiram as the power that makes the
round. The finding of the three ruffians. The three burials of
Hiram. The raising by King Solomon. The monument at the
place of burial. Raising of the candidate. The three columns.
The forty-seventh problem of Euclid.*

The remaining portion of the initiation is a masonic
drama, representing the life, death and resurrection
of Hiram Abiff, whose part the candidate is made to take.
Hiram was the master builder of King Solomon's Temple
and was slain by workmen for his refusal to impart the
Word to them, and after two burials was raised by King
Solomon and then buried the third time. This story conceals
the great lesson of Masonry.

Hiram is the seminal principle, the generative power,
the sex power, not an organ, not the fluid, but the power,
invisible and most mysterious. This power lies in the
Conscious Light of the Intelligence which is carried
by desire and is an extract from the four elements,
prepared by the four systems of the body. This power,
having therefore something of the seven faculties of the
Intelligence, something of the three parts of the Triune
Self, and something of the four elements, is to be found
only in a human body. This power is concentrated monthly
by the inner brain, so becomes the lunar germ, and as
such descends along the sympathetic nervous system in the
front of the body and gathers Light of the Intelligence as
it proceeds. The lunar germ in man is a concentration of
the whole power, but one half of the power is checked in
its possible development. A man, symbolized according to

the language for which the masonic word Geometry stands, by the triangle Cancer, Scorpio and Pisces, has only half the power, and so has a woman, symbolized by the female triangle Taurus, Virgo and Capricorn. The other half in each is dormant or suppressed. The active half develops in the body organs to express itself and is lost through them. With this loss are mingled thoughts of lust, violence, shame, dishonor, disease, love and hate, which are the cable-tow of rebirth. If Hiram is not lost, but is saved, the half of him that is checked will develop in the body and there will build new parts, new organs, new channels. Hiram is the builder.

Hiram, the Master-Builder, the Grand Master, draws his designs on the trestle-board—that is, the lines on the breath-form which is in the sympathetic nervous system—and passes out each day, that is, each life, through the South gate, Libra, of the outer courts of the Temple. That is to say, the monthly germ is lost. It is his usual custom to enter the unfinished Sanctum Sanctorum, that is, the heart and lungs, on the line Cancer to Capricorn. There thinking draws out the lines of his designs upon the trestle-board, whereby the craft pursue their labors, that is, whereby the workmen or elementals in the four systems of the body build according to the lines, the physical state and circumstances in which the body exists.

On one day, that is, in one life, when Hiram, following his usual custom attempts to leave the body at the South gate, the gate of sex, he is hindered and restrained from going out. He turns, seeks to go out at the West gate, Cancer, and is again prevented. Then he seeks the East gate, Capricorn, and there he is slain. This means that the sex power sought to leave by the sex opening and when that was barred, by the opening in the breasts, that is, by emotions, and when that was closed, by a place in the spine, which stands for the brain or intellect, and when that exit, too, was blocked, it died to these mortal expressions of itself. Having so died to mortality and corruption it was raised to build an incorruptible and immortal body.

The three ruffians Jubela, Jubelo and Jubelum, are no ruffians, but are the Junior Warden, Senior Warden and Worshipful Master, the three officers of the lodge, in

Masonry, and they stand also for the three parts of the Triune Self, Jubela being the Doer, Jubelo the Thinker, and Jubelum the Knower. Each has a part of the Word. If their parts were combined they would be AUM or AOM or three of the four parts of the Word. But no combination is made, that is, the three parts do not work coordinately.

Hiram has the Word, he is the Word, for he has the Light, that is, the Intelligence powers and the Triune Self powers and the powers of the four elements, and he has them combined. When assaulted by the first ruffian and asked for the Word, Hiram, therefore, says: "Wait until the Temple is completed," that is, until he has built the immortal body. He says about giving the secrets of the Word: "I cannot; nor can they be given, except in the presence of Solomon, King of Israel (the Knower), and Hiram, King of Tyre (the Thinker), and myself" The Doer (the Light in the sex with feeling-and-desire). This means that the Word cannot be imparted by the sex power since the sex power only builds the immortal body, the Temple. When Hiram as the combined powers of the Light, the Doer and the sexes, has completed the building of the body he can act his own part as Hiram, the Doer of feeling-and-desire. Then together with the Thinker, King of Tyre, and the Knower, Solomon, he is the Word and enters the finished Temple.

Hiram is many things. He is the mysterious creative power hidden in the powers of the sexes, hence he is the builder, the Master Builder; he is the Lost Word, being the Doer which is lost, because it is immersed in flesh and blood and does not know itself in the human being; and he is the combined powers of the Light and of the Triune Self and of the nature powers of the sexes when he has found himself in the ruins of the temple and is conscious of himself as the Triune Self.

Jubela, Jubelo and Jubelum are ruffians in so far as they are not performing the true functions of their offices. They are said to be ruffians because they act as the Doer part in its Thinker and Knower aspects, when it is the false "I." The three are only the Doer part in the three aspects of its Triune Self. Jubela gives Hiram a blow with the gauge, a tool of the Apprentice, across the throat, according to the ritual. This is a blind for the sex part. Jubelo strikes

Hiram with the square, a tool of the Fellow Craft, across the breast, and Jubelum fells him with a setting-maul, the gavel of a Master. The gauge is the line, the square the surface, and the maul the cube.

Hiram has so far gone out of the South gate, his custom in the bodies of the run of human beings. The masonic drama refers to a time when it is discovered that the sex power holds the key to all secrets and to all power. To wrest the key from this power the human being restrains it from going out. Mere restraint does not obtain the secret, but the power, when controlled, rises, passing from the sex functions into the four physical bodies. Then the human being prevents Hiram from leaving by thoughts, at the emotional center. But Hiram does not yield the secret, because the human being practices the restraint from selfish motives to get power, and not to rebuild the Temple, and because the human being is physically and psychically incapable of holding the power. Hiram passes to the East and there meets Jubelum who, though in the true aspect he is the Knower, is in the drama the false "I," an egotistical aspect of the Doer. To him Hiram cannot impart the Word. Yet, the human being, though from selfish motives, has so far advanced that there is no more physical reproduction. This is symbolized by the slaying of Hiram.

In the conspiracy to obtain the secret of Hiram were fifteen workmen. Twelve recanted and the remaining three, Jubela, Jubelo and Jubelum, carried out the plot. The twelve here are the twelve points on the Zodiac in the body, the three are the double aspects of the Doer, and the body-mind. The twelve represent numbers, that is, twelve ultimate beings and orders of beings.

Everything in the manifested Universe is in some measure representative of the Great Twelve. The human body is their organ. The more a human being develops, the more will he have in him live centers representing and responding to the Great Twelve. King Solomon sends the twelve workmen in the body in search of the ruffians. He sends three East, three North, three South, and three West. He sends Taurus, Virgo and Capricorn to act in the East, Leo, Sagittary and Aries in the North, Aquarius, Gemini and Libra in the South, and Scorpio, Pisces and Cancer in the West. Of these triads, those of Leo, Aries, and Sagittary, and of Gemini, Libra and Aquarius are universal, the first triangle operating through the second. The triad of Taurus, Virgo and Capricorn operates through that of Cancer, Scorpio and Pisces, and both are human. Each pair of triads forms a six-pointed star. There is the universal hexad, the macrocosm, and the human hexad, the microcosm. The universal hexad, composed of the sexless triad, Aries, Leo, Sagittary and the androgynous triad, Gemini, Libra and Aquarius, is God or Supreme Intelligence, and nature. The human hexad is composed of the Cancer, Scorpio and Pisces triad, pointing West, which is man or the male triad, and of Taurus, Virgo and Capricorn, pointing East, which is woman, the female triad.

The macrocosmic and the microcosmic signs are represented in the human body by twelve parts and centers, each having its special character. The human body therefore is potentially a complete universe. The six universal signs are centers at which the six human signs can act if the human signs come together in any one of those six. For instance, if the male and female triads unite at their points of Scorpio and Virgo in Libra, they procreate through the universal gate of sex of the nature triad. But if the male and female triads at their points of Scorpio and Capricorn unite at Sagittary, the sexless gate of the universal triad, they create a thought. Though the twelve powers are represented in a human body, they cannot act freely and fully, but are restrained, paralyzed, half dead, impotent, except the powers represented by Virgo, Scorpio, and Libra, that is, the female in a female body, the male in a male body, and the sex in both bodies.

Hiram is the power that makes the rounds of the twelve centers, that strengthens and empowers them, builds up the twelve centers, makes them alive and fits them so that they can be related to the Great Twelve, and so that the Doer in the body can act with the Great Twelve.

King Solomon's sending the twelve workmen in search of the three ruffians means that after Hiram is slain, within the meaning of the legend, the Knower part which is in contact with the body commands the twelve powers in the body to locate the three ruffians who have brought

24

about the death of Hiram, who are the false "I" in its three aspects. The three ruffians are found near the body of the slain, that is, the physical suppression of the sex power, and are executed. They are condemned for having tried to get the power from Hiram before they were qualified to receive it.

Hiram was buried three times. First the ruffians buried him in the rubbish of the Temple, that is, the sex power was turned into the foods of the body to build it up. At night they came back to give the body a more decent burial. They carried it West, to the brow of the hill West of Mount Moriah, that is, the sex power was buried in or turned into psychic power. There it was discovered by a party of workmen. After it had been raised by King Solomon himself by the strong grip or lion's paw—which is the grip identified with a life like that of Jesus, the lion of the Tribe of Judah so-called from the alleged heraldic lion of the Tribe—it was buried near the Sanctum Sanctorum of King Solomon's Temple, that is, the sex power was turned into the spine.

The raising by Solomon is significant. The body could not be raised by the grip of the Entered Apprentice, nor by that of the Fellow Craft, that is the Doer could not, either with the psychic or its mental aspect raise or transmute the mortal into an immortal body. It required the Knower, here King Solomon himself, to raise Hiram. King Solomon had the assistance of Hiram, King of Tyre, the Thinker, and of the brethren, that is, the powers in the body.

The tradition of Masonry is that a monument was erected to the memory of Hiram, at his place of burial. The monument represents a virgin weeping over a broken column. Before her was an open book, behind her stood Time. It is a reminder of the destruction of the original temple, at which the Boaz column, which represented the female column in the temple of man was broken. The vestige or monument is the sternum, which is all that is left. The virgin is the woman weeping over her own broken column. Time is death, as the continuous passing of the events; and the open book is the breath-form and aia, which bear the record of what happened. The female figure is also the widow, as the broken column, who was the mother of

Hiram, weeping for the male power, which she lost when the column was broken. Hiram is the son of a widow; he is unprotected and has had to wander along the labyrinth of the alimentary canal since the column was broken.

The destruction of the temple occurs in every life. Hiram is not allowed to rebuild it. In this sense he is slain in every life. At each life he is resurrected and tries to rebuild the temple beginning with the re-establishment of the column, which is broken. The Monument of the woman with her broken column is a reminder that a Mason must re-establish the broken column in himself as the requisite to rebuild his temple, and he can re-establish the column only by keeping Hiram in the body to rebuild it. Hiram has within him the original plan of the immortal body which, when rebuilt, will be greater than the first temple.

The candidate having been made to take the part of Hiram is finally raised by King Solomon, the Master of the Lodge, by the real grip of a Master Mason, and on the five points of fellowship, or five points of the body. The brethren assist in raising the candidate to a standing position. The hoodwink is slipped off his eyes. After he has received an historical account of the events he passed through as Hiram, the Master explains the various symbols. He uses them as subjects for moral exhortations and rules.

The three grand masonic columns or pillars, designated Wisdom, Strength, and Beauty, stand for the three parts of the body. They also stand for parts of the Triune Self. In this connection the pillar of Wisdom is Solomon, the spinal or Jachin column; the pillar of Strength is Hiram, King of Tyre, the sympathetic or Boaz column; and the pillar of Beauty is Hiram Abiff, the bridge or bridge builder, between the two.

The forty-seventh problem of Euclid is more than a moral exhortation. It means that when the male (desire) and the female (feeling) in one physical body work together they build a new body equal to their sum. The new body, the square of the hypotenuse, is the temple rebuilt.

After the candidate has been raised to the degree of Master Mason, he represents the Doer, Thinker, and Knower, each developed to its capacity and coordinated so that they are a trinity, the Triune Self. This trinity is in Masonry represented as a right-angled triangle in the lodge.

SECTION 5

Meaning of the lodge as a room and as the brothers. The officers, their stations and duties. The three degrees as the foundation of Masonry. The work. A Mason's own lodge.

The lodge as a room or hall is an oblong square, which is a half of a perfect square, and which is inside or outside the lower half of a circle. Each lodge meets in the same room, alike furnished, but the lodge working in the Apprentice degree is styled the Ground Floor, the lodge working the Fellow Craft degree is called the Middle Chamber, and the lodge working the Master degree is called the Sanctum Sanctorum, all in King Solomon's Temple. The lodge in this sense symbolizes, with the present day humanity, the part of the body from the breasts and from the back opposite the breasts to the sex. When the temple is rebuilt the Ground Floor will be the pelvic section, the Middle Chamber the abdominal section, and the Sanctum Sanctorum the thoracic section.

The lodge, as a number of brothers who compose it, represents certain working centers and their activities in the body of a Mason. These are shown by the officers stationed in the West, South and East. These are the three without whom there can be no lodge. The breasts, standing for the Boaz column, where the sternum is, are the station of the Senior Warden in the West. The places of the coccygeal gland and anus, which are the ends of the two tubes, are the station of the Junior Warden in the South. A place in the spinal cord opposite the heart is the station of the Master in the East.

The Senior Deacon in front of and to the right of the Master, and the Junior Deacon at the right and in front of the Senior Warden make five, and the Secretary at the left and the Treasurer at the right of the Master, make seven. These are the seven officers of the lodge. In addition there are the two stewards, one on each side of the Junior Warden in the South, and the Tyler, the guard at the door.

The Senior Warden's duty is to strengthen and support the Master and assist him in carrying on the work of the lodge.

The Junior Warden's duty, according to the ritual, is to observe and record the time, to call the craft from labor to refreshment, to superintend that, to keep them from intemperance or excess and to call them to labor again. His station is there but there is no organ or conduit from Boaz to Jachin. His duty is to observe the time, that is, sun time, the Master standing for the sun, and moon time, the Senior Warden for the moon. This relates to sex power, the moon, and to Doer power, the sun, that is to say, the duty of that center is to observe the time and the seasons of the lunar and solar germs. He should call the craft, that is, the Masons working in the part of the temple called the lodge, and the elemental workmen who labor outside, in the quarries, in other parts of the body. The four senses and the elementals in the systems all go to the sex center to get refreshment. The center of the Junior Warden should balance the forces of Boaz and Jachin and with these forces refresh the workmen of the temple.

"As the sun rises in the East to open and govern the day, so rises the Master in the East to open and govern his lodge, set the craft to work and give them proper instructions," says the ritual. The Master is the sun, represented by the solar germ, in the body, as the Senior Warden is the moon. The Master dispenses his light from his seat in the East, that is, the spinal cord back of the heart, to the Senior Warden at the breasts, through whom his orders are issued.

The remaining officers of the lodge, considered as centers in the body, are assistants to these three main officers, near whom they are stationed and whose orders they execute. The Secretary and Treasurer record and keep on the breath-form the accounts of the transactions of the lodge, which are carried over from lodge to lodge, that is from life to life.

The lodge as a number of brothers who compose it stands also for the embodied Doer portions or contacts of the Triune Self and their aspects. The Junior Warden is the Doer and his two stewards are the active and the passive side of desire-and-feeling. The Senior Warden represents the Thinker and the Junior Deacon is the active side, called reason. The Master is the Knower and the Senior Deacon is I-ness, the passive aspect. It may be noted that the Senior Warden and the Master have each only one assistant.

The degrees of Entered Apprentice, Fellow Craft and Master Mason, are the foundations of Masonry, which is the building of an immortal body. The Entered Apprentice is the Doer, the Fellow Craft the Thinker, and the Master Mason the Knower in contact with the body. They carry on the work of the lodge in the trunk of the body and are assisted by the other officers. The work of the lodge is kept before the eyes of Masons by the opening of the lodge, the order of business, the initiating, passing and raising of candidates and the closing of the lodge. All is done with impressiveness and becoming dignity. The real work is the initiating, passing and raising of the Doer-in-the-body to conscious relation with its Thinker and Knower parts.

Every Mason should open his own lodge, that is, begin in the morning the work of the day with the dignity of the opening of his masonic lodge. He should recognize the stations and duties of the parts and their centers in the body and charge them to see that the workmen, that is, the elementals functioning in the body, are properly employed. He should recognize that he is the candidate to be initiated by the trials of the day, and that he must pass through them with temperance, fortitude, prudence and justice, so that he may be exalted and receive more Light.

SECTION 6

The cable-tow. The Royal Arch. The candidate as the keystone.
Realization of the great Masonic symbol. The fifth degree. The
fourth degree. The keystone with the mark of Hiram. The sixth
degree. Another aspect of the keystone symbol. The union of
Boaz and Jachin. The Glory of the Lord fills the Lord's house.
The seventh degree. The Tabernacle. The Master's jewels and
the Ark of the Covenant. The Name and the Word.

The cable-tow of the four senses leads the candidate
(the Doer-in-the-body) through each of the four great
degrees of Masonry, until the senses cease to be ties. The
Master Mason receives More Light in the Chapter or Holy
Royal Arch, which is in the North. This is the Fourth
Degree. The Lodge is an oblong square in the lower half
of the circle; the Chapter is another oblong square, which
together with the first, forms a perfect square, within the
circle, and that part of the circle which is the arc above or
North of this square, is the Royal Arch. Into that, when the
cable-tow no longer leads him the candidate is fitted as a
keystone. This Fourth Degree has, however, in the course of
time been stretched out and cut into four degrees, of which
the Fourth, Sixth, and Seventh Degrees contain the work
of the original Fourth Degree.

The Royal Arch is the culmination and consummation
of the three degrees of Entered Apprentice, Fellow Craft
and Master Mason. The great Masonic symbol of compass
and square is there realized. The three points of the square
are those three lower degrees, and the compass, so joined
with them as to make a six-pointed star, now, in the Royal
Arch Degrees, represent the Light of the Intelligence, which
in the Conscious Light of the Royal Arch Mason is the
threefold Light that has come into his noetic, his mental
and his psychic atmospheres. This state of a Mason is the
subject of which various aspects are symbolized by the work
of the Fourth, Sixth and Seventh Degrees, relating to the
Light of the Intelligence when the Glory of the Lord fills

31

the House, to the keystone when the arch is completed, to the Word when it is found, and to the Name when the divided Adam or Jehovah becomes one.

In the Fifth Degree, that of Past Master, the candidate takes the obligation of a Master of the Lodge, and upon being installed is made to see and feel his inability to keep the turbulent brethren sufficiently in order to conduct the work of the Lodge. This degree is a mere filler for ceremonial purposes.

The Fourth Degree or that of Mark Master is said to have been instituted by King Solomon for the purpose of detecting impostors. Each workman was required to put his distinctive mark upon the product of his labor. The Mark Master could thereby detect impostors and could notice unfinished and imperfect work. This degree is dedicated to Hiram, the builder, and its characteristic is the keystone he had fashioned and on which was his mark. This stone possessing merits unknown to the builders was rejected by them but became the "chief stone of the corner."

In the lodge in which the Master Mason is to be advanced to the Fourth, or honorary, Degree of Mark Master, the brethren, during the opening, gather round a miniature of King Solomon's Temple,—symbol of the temple into which they are to rebuild their bodies—which is erected on the middle of the floor. During the opening the Master says to them: "Ye also, as living stones, be ye built up a spiritual house, an holy priesthood, to offer up sacrifices acceptable to God."

The candidate being duly and truly prepared and carrying a keystone is conducted into the lodge. Two of the brethren who carry oblong stones, and the candidate with his keystone, present the stones as specimens of their work. The two stones carried by the companions are received for the temple, but the keystone, being neither oblong nor square, is rejected as of no account and is heaved over among the rubbish of the temple where Hiram was buried at one time. For want of a keystone to one of the principal arches the workmen are disturbed. The Right Worshipful Master, representing King Solomon, says that he gave Hiram Abiff, the Grand Master, orders to make that keystone, previous to his assassination, and inquires if such a stone has not been brought up for inspection. The keystone which the candidate had brought and had seen heaved over into the rubbish, is found and is now received and becomes the "head of the corner."

The keystone has on it the mark of Hiram. The keystone is Hiram transformed into a certain lunar germ, which was preserved, died to the world, rose along the spine, and ascended into the head. Hiram's mark is a double cross made by a stationary cross H.S.W.K. and a movable cross T.T.S.S. The import of these crosses can be known by the meaning of the Zodiacal signs which these eight points of the crosses represent on the circumference of the circle. His mark is his new name, a name of an Order of beings to which he now belongs. This new name is written on a white stone, or the purified essence, that is the vesture of Hiram. Hiram, having overcome, has eaten of the hidden manna, that is, has received the Light accumulated by successive lunar germs. The keystone that has the mark of Hiram, also stands for the candidate himself who has overcome, who has ascended into the hill of the Lord and who shall stand in his holy place.

The Sixth Degree, that of the Most Excellent Master, is the initiation of the candidate by the descent of the Light into the completed temple, or, in Masonic language, when the Glory of the Lord fills the House. In his obligation the candidate promises that he will dispense light and knowledge to all ignorant and uninformed brethren.

Another aspect of the keystone is emphasized by the ceremonies which take up again the teaching of the stone with Hiram's mark, that is, the candidate himself. The ceremonies now represent the day for the celebration of the capstone, copestone, or keystone. The keystone is made to close an arch placed on the two columns Boaz and Jachin. This is a symbol that the physical body has been rebuilt, that an arch over Boaz and Jachin unites them above and another arch unites them below. This is done as the result of the action of the Junior Warden in the first three degrees. He harmonized the male and female forces in the West and East columns, at the South, Libra, and with these equilibrated forces built the arches, or bridges, below and above. With the arch above and the keystone inserted therein, the temple is completed.

The Light of the Intelligence descends into the candidate and fills his body. The Glory of the Lord fills the Lord's House. The mortal body has been transformed into an immortal body. This culmination of the Masonic purpose is sometimes represented by the fire coming down from heaven and by a temple in the lodge being filled with effulgent light. Sometimes a passage from the Bible is read and an illumination made to show to the candidate the lodge filled with the glory that floods the temple.

In the Seventh Degree or Royal Arch are symbolized events which preceded the completion of the temple, and some information is given about the Word.

The candidate is made to represent one of three Masons who after the destruction of Jerusalem by Nebuchadnezzar were captives in Babylon till Cyrus of Persia liberated them. They returned to Jerusalem to assist in building the temple. On arrival they found the Tabernacle, a temporary structure. This is the temporary physical body, which serves until the temple is rebuilt. The three were given tools and directed to begin their labors at the North East corner of the ruined temple. There they discovered a secret vault under a trap which was the keystone of an arch. The keystone taken before the Grand Council was there discovered to be the keystone of the principal arch in Solomon's Temple. Lowered by cable-tow into the vault the candidate finds three small trying-squares which are by the Grand Council recognized as the Master's Jewels of King Solomon, of King Hiram of Tyre and of Hiram Abiff. On another descent a small box is found which is recognized by the Grand Council as the Ark of the Covenant. Out of this chest are taken a pot of manna and four pieces of paper containing in right angles and dots the key to a mystery language. With this key three mysterious words written in triangular form upon the Ark, become readable as the name of God in the Chaldaic, Hebrew and Syriac languages; and this Name of the Deity is in the ritual said to be the long lost Master Mason's Word or Logos. This identification among modern Masons of the Name and the Word is a blind, or is due to a mistake.

The Name and the Word are distinct and not the same. The Name is a name, one of the names, of the God of the physical world, the Earth Spirit. This God belongs to the nature-side. It is known by different names in different ages among different peoples. Brahma is one of the names; originally it was Brahm and after it divided it became Brahma, and then the Trimurti Brahma-Vishnu-Shiva. This is the Name of the God of the physical world, with the Hindus. The name of the Triune Self, however, is BrahmA, VishnU, BrahM, the last letters of which are the Word.

The Hebrew Name is Jehovah, and modern Masons have adopted this. It is a name of the ruler of the physical world and its four planes. This God has no physical body except the formless four elements in the physical world and the human bodies of those who are born in his Name and who obey his laws. At one time this God acted through human physical bodies which were sexless, then he acted through human bodies which were bisexual, and now he acts through human bodies that are male human bodies and that are female human bodies. The Name can be pronounced only when a human body has in it active masculine and passive feminine powers. A man can only give half of the Name, because his body is only half the Name. To this fact refers the Masonic practice of saying: "I will letter it or halve it." The Name is the name of the body and the body must be rebuilt into a balanced male-female body before it is the Name and the dweller in the body can breathe the Name. The Name belongs to the body, is of the four elements and hence has four letters, Jod, He, Vav, He. The Name is ineffable until such time as it can be breathed by the dweller in a normal balanced or sexless physical body.

The Word, an English translation of the Logos, as used by St. John, is not the Name. It is an expression of the full Triune Self powers, each of the three parts being represented in it by a sound, and the perfect body in which the Triune Self dwells being also represented by a sound. The Doer part is expressed as A, the Thinker part as U or O, the Knower part as M, and the perfect body as I. The Word is I-A-O-M, in four syllables or letters. The expression of the perfect body and the Triune Self as these sounds is an expression of the Conscious Light of the Intelligence through that Self and body. When a part in its physical body sounds as IAOM each of the parts sounds AOM, and each represents a Logos. The Knower is then the First Logos, the Thinker the Second Logos and the Doer the Third Logos.

The Word is symbolized by a circle in which are a hexad of two interlaced triangles, and the point in the center. The point is the M, the triangle Aries, Leo, Sagittary is the A, the triangle Gemini, Libra, Aquarius is the U or the O, and the circle is the fully expressed point M as well as the line of the body I. The hexad is made up of the macrocosmic signs standing for the sexless triad and the androgynous triad, the triangle of God as Intelligence and the triangle of God as nature. These letters in which the perfect Self sounds, are symbolized in Masonry by the square and compass or the emblem of the interlaced triangles.

There is a succinct relationship of the Word with the Ineffable Name. The Word is feeling-and-desire, the Doer. The Doer is lost in the body of flesh and blood in the world of life and death. Thus the Doer is the *lost Word*. The body, when perfected, serves as the instrument through which the Doer pronounces the *Ineffable Name*. The *Ineffable Name* and the embodied *Word*, when one is fitted to speak it, is IAOM. By so doing the body is raised from a horizontal to an upright position.

The Name is pronounced as follows: It is started by opening the lips with an "ee" sound graduating into a broad "a" as the mouth opens wider with the lips forming an oval shape and then graduating the sound to "o" as the lips form a circle, and again modulating to an "m" sound as the lips close to a point. This point resolves itself to a point within the head.

Expressed phonetically the Name is "EE-Ah-Oh-Mmm" and is pronounced with one continuous outbreathing with a slight nasal tone in the manner described above. It can be correctly and properly expressed with its full power only by one who has brought his physical body to a state of perfection, that is, balanced and sexless.

SECTION 7

Summary of the teachings of Masonry. They center around "Light." The symbols, acts and words of the ritual. Ritualists and their workings. The permanent forms of Masonry and twisted teachings. Scriptural passages. Geometrical symbols. Their value. Masonry has in trust certain geometrical symbols which, coordinated in a system for the Masonic work, are thus preserved.

The teachings of Masonry are few and definite. They are of the Supreme Intelligence, of the Light of the original state of the Triune Self, of the first body when the Doer was without sin and the body lived in the Light, of the death of the body, which is called the destruction of the temple, of the duty to rebuild the temple, of the training of the Doer of feeling-and-desire, as the candidate, to be conscious of itself in the body and to come into conscious relation with the Thinker and the Knower, which training is symbolized by the degrees of the Entered Apprentice, the Fellow Craft and the Master Mason, that is, the three parts of the Triune Self, of the sex power, called Hiram Abiff, by which the temple is rebuilt or the body made immortal, and of the Light filling the temple. The Masonic teachings center around the Light, the Conscious Light the Doer had, the Light it had lost and the Light it must regain. "More light" is the true Masonic prayer. Getting light is the phrase used in Masonry for becoming conscious in higher degrees. Masons take their obligations of virtue and holiness to get more light, to become children of Light.

The symbols, the symbolic acts and the words of the ritual do not always present these teachings. In the course of time and with the popularization of Masonry, some of these teachings have become obscured because of twisting, substituting and adding symbols and work. Various ritualists have been active, not always within the bounds or along the lines of the Masonic landmarks. Nevertheless, the fundamental forms remain, and show the misfits. The

Doer, Thinker, and Knower parts are symbolized by the Junior Warden, Senior Warden, and Worshipful Master, by Jubela, Jubelo, and Jubelum, by the Entered Apprentice, the Fellow Craft, and the Master Mason, by Hiram Abiff, Hiram, King of Tyre, and King Solomon, by the Pillars of Beauty, Strength, and Wisdom. Where the same three parts are symbolized and there is an omission, it is clear that the later ritualists worked without understanding the relation of the three parts of the Triune Self. So the sun and the moon stand for the body and the feeling, but there is nothing for the desire in this imagery unless it be the stars, and in their place the ritual for the Entered Apprentice degree mentions the Master of the Lodge. Desire should be the Master of the Lodge in that degree. Boaz symbolizes the Thinker and Jachin the Knower, but there is nothing in the ritual to stand for the balancer, the Doer, which makes the arch below, corresponding to the Royal Arch above. However, notwithstanding twists, missing links and the use of the same symbol to indicate different subjects, the general forms of Masonry remain as guides, to which the growth of rites, orders and symbology is reduced from time to time.

Among the permanent forms of Masonry are the point in the circle, the oblong square or the form of the lodge, the right-angled triangle or the square, the equilateral triangle which is the symbol of the Supreme Intelligence, the compass as the symbol of the light coming down, the interlaced triangles, the two columns, the three Great Lights, the arch, the keystone with the two crosses, the white lambskin or apron, the cable-tow, the four degrees and the Master Builder. At such times much stress is laid on some of these symbols, at other times symbols like the trestle-board, the G or point in the circle, the All-seeing Eye as the symbol of the Supreme Intelligence, the source of all Light, and the Blazing Star, symbol of the teacher of the Messianic cycle, are made less important according to the understanding and fancy of the ritualists. Notwithstanding the warning against any change or removal of the ancient landmarks, Masons vary the ritual. Thus many of the teachings have become twisted. For instance, the fire which is a symbol of Jehovah is identified with the Light, which is representative of the Supreme Intelligence; the cardinal point, the North, through which the Light comes, has disappeared from the ritual and the North is dark; the Word is confounded with the Name; the explanation why the three officers act as three ruffians has disappeared. Much of this deterioration is due to the fact that Scriptural passages which are parts of the ritual, are interpreted according to the religious sentiment of the times, and so color, distort or hide the Masonic teachings which the symbols preserve.

Masons have long been in a time of darkness. They are perhaps to be excused for the loss of the light in a time of general darkness. In the present age, however, if they are traveling in search of light, if light is the object of their search, they can find it by searching for it through their symbols. They will get more light if they try to hold the Conscious Light in thinking steadily on the meaning of their symbols.

A geometrical symbol expresses an idea and is a prototype for thinking. It is the original pattern after which other things are modeled, by which they are prefigured, predetermined and given identity, to which they correspond and to which they respond. All things can be epitomized and placed under a few prototypes from which they have originated and by which they are predetermined. Therefore, physical things can be summarized under abstractions which are symbolic. Symbols show a unity in diversity.

Many things can be used as symbols, but geometrical symbols are the highest, because they are best adapted to convey the idea that is expressed in them. The reason is that the body-mind, feeling-mind, and desire-mind work with points, lines, angles and curves, that geometrical forms are the simplest, the most direct and freest from irregularities and complications, and that, therefore, the functions of the three minds are at home with geometrical symbols and get from them without color, form, prejudice, variations and coverings, the essence in the idea or thought which the symbols convey. Points and lines are not seen on the physical plane. Matter on the physical plane appears in forms. These forms have outlines, that is, they end. Lines are conceptions, due to the functions of the feeling-mind and have no physical, tangible existence. They exist on the life plane of the physical world. Points and lines are the matter on the life plane, that is, if the matter on this plane could be seen or conceived, it would be to the average human understanding as points, lines, angles and curves. With this kind of matter, that is, points, lines, angles and curves, the body-mind can work. In order to get the meaning of anything that is not physical the body-mind thinks in points and lines.

A geometrical symbol is not colored, but everything in the world that is seen is colored and therefore does not show the truth, which is without color. True form is without color. Geometrical symbols are true forms. They show the actual character of the things they represent. The reason people cannot use geometrical symbols is that they are looking at the colored forms of nature and have to grow accustomed to geometrical symbols before they can use them and see through them. They first suggest and then reveal the idea they express. When a human thinks intentionally through geometrical symbols he can get the truth which the symbols contain.

All geometrical symbols have their origin in points, lines, angles and curves which receive their value as symbols from positions they hold in the circle. The Zodiac is the best symbol of the circle with the twelve points on the circumference which give a value to geometrical symbols. The value which the symbols so receive is given them by their position relative to the twelve points. Masonry has its symbols from the Zodiac.

The chief reason Masonry exists, and has been preserved when other secret bodies have perished, is that it has in trust certain symbols and that these are coordinated and vitalized in a system for Masonic work. These symbols are geometrical. If Masonic symbols are tools, emblems or buildings, they are valuable because of the geometrical lines they embody.

———————

Masons who have read the foregoing approved it, and it is now published with the hope that all readers will see its application to "The Great Way" described in *Thinking and Destiny*, and which preceded this work in the original manuscript. It is addressed to all human beings, and the author, though not a member of the Masonic Fraternity, wishes especially to remind all Masons, of whatever Lodge or Rite, that entrusted to their care were the plans for the rebuilding of their second temple which will be greater than the first temple that they destroyed in the long-ago-at-the-beginning of time.

The information for the building of an immortal physical body has been a closely guarded secret preserved through all the ages by the Masonic Fraternity. The works of the author are for the purpose of showing every human being, regardless of race, creed, or color, who really desires to return to and re-establish his Father's house in The Realm of Permanence may begin the Great Work without being crushed by the weight of the world's thought. That is to say, without having to leave his active work and retire from the world to do it in secret.

It is possible, but not probable, that human beings can rebuild their temples in the present life. However, anyone may prepare himself and become an entered apprentice and take as many degrees as he can in the present life and continue the work in the next life on earth.

This article also is to remind all Masons that it is *their* work. Let those, who will, see.

H. W. P.

SYMBOLS AND ILLUSTRATIONS

LEGEND TO SYMBOLS

Masonic Lodges: Entered Apprentice, Fellow Craft, Master Mason, and Royal Arch degrees, showing the stations or gates of Cancer (♋) the senior warden in the West; Libra (♎) the junior warden in the South; and Capricorn (♑) the master in the East; in each of the degrees. The physical body of man is the ground floor or plan or lodge in which all the degrees are worked, as the body or lodge is prepared for each degree.

The conscious self, as the Doer-in-the-body, is the entered apprentice to be initiated in the first degree. He begins to learn the use of his rule, or line of feeling, from Cancer to Libra (♋ to ♎) and his line of desire from Libra to Capricorn (♎ to ♑). When he has brought these into right relationship to each other they unite and make the square on which a Mason works, and the oblong square (♋ to ♎ to ♑) below. The feeling line and desire line make the square of the right-angled triangle (the hypotenuse), the square of all true Masons on which the work of the lodge is conducted.

All degrees are degrees to be taken by the Doer-in-the-body; not by the Thinker and Knower. They await the Doer on his initiation as a Master Mason. The Doer is initiated into the higher degrees to be eventually united with the Thinker and Knower in the Royal Arch. Then they will be complete and perfect. The work of the Doer as entered apprentice is, as he advances by degrees, to rebuild his present physical body into that temple not made with hands, immortal in The Eternal.

This figure shows the Masonic Lodge to be the present physical body. The oblong square is given in detail. The two columns and the three pillars are, by extension, also shown.

The Groundfloor is the pelvic section. The Middle

Chamber is the abdominal section. The Sanctum Sanctorum is the thoracic section. The Royal Arch is the physical body in its atmospheres, complete. The top of the head represents the keystone.

Refer to symbols, pages 945, 960, 961, in *Thinking and Destiny*. On page 961, Fig. VI-B shows the front, or nature, column of the perfect body—which is now broken, being absent below the sternum. *(This information can now be found on pages 46–48 of this book.—Ed.)*

The three signs Cancer, Leo, Virgo (♋ , ♌ , ♍) are the three female signs, from the breasts to the womb; when squared, 3 x 3, they make 9. The male signs are four, Libra, Scorpio, Sagittary, Capricorn (♎ , ♏ , ♐ , ♑), from the coccyx Libra to Capricorn opposite the heart. When squared they equal 16. 9 plus 16 equal 25. The five signs, Aquarius (♒), Pisces (♓), Aries (♈), Taurus (♉), Gemini (♊), are signs representing the hypotenuse, above Cancer (♋) and Capricorn (♑) which when squared equal 25, the square of the circle, thus "squaring the circle."

H. W. P.
New York City
December 1, 1951

44

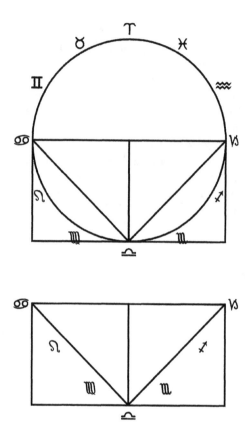

The Oblong Square

The lower section is set apart to show the Oblong Square itself. The first three signs, Cancer, Virgo, Leo are feminine and the next four, Libra, Scorpio, Sagittary, Capricorn, are masculine. The sum of the squares of the first three and the next four is equal to the square of the hypotenuse which, itself, is actually equal to five and conforms to the five unmanifested signs representing the Royal Arch. As is readily seen in the plate, the hypotenuse is equal to one side of the square capable of encompassing the circle. It is the total sum of the Mason's work on the Oblong Square, the trestle-board, his lodge, his body, which squares the circle and enables him to take his rightful place as the Keystone in The Royal Arch in The Realm of Permanence.

The following pages of symbols and illustrations (including Fig. I-E, referred to below) are from the Symbols, Illustrations and Charts section of Thinking and Destiny.—*Ed*

THE PHYSICAL PLANE OF THE HUMAN
PHYSICAL WORLD
and its
FOUR STATES OF MATTER

Fig. I-D

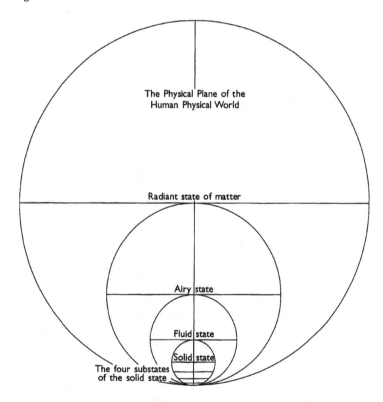

In the four substates of the solid state are the stars, sun, moon, and the earth, (Fig. I-E).

*   *   *

All these states are invisible to the human eye, but some of the objects in the four substates of the solid state can be perceived by the human.

46

SPINAL CORD
and
SPINAL NERVES

SPINAL COLUMN
and
SPINAL CORD

Fig. VI-A, b

Fig. VI-A, d

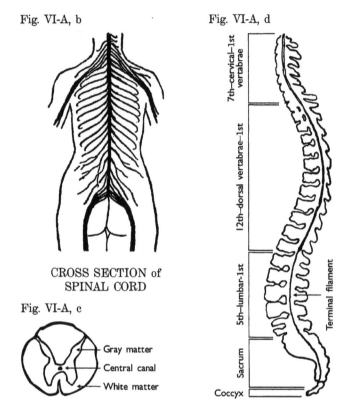

CROSS SECTION of
SPINAL CORD

Fig. VI-A, c

Gray matter

Central canal

White matter

7th-cervical-1st vertabrae

12th-dorsal vertabrae-1st

5th-lumbar-1st

Sacrum

Coccyx

Terminal filament

THE SPINAL CORD
AND ITS RELATION TO THE SPINAL COLUMN

The spinal cord proper reaches from the base of the brain to about the junction of the 12th dorsal and the 1st lumbar vertebrae; its prolongation downward is called the terminal filament, which is anchored below to the coccyx. The spinal cord has a central canal, the prolongation downward of the ventricles of the brain; below, in the embryo, this canal reaches to the end of the terminal filament, but in the adult it usually becomes clogged up within the filament and disappears more or less, in the run of human beings.

The spinal column is divided into five sections: the cervical, dorsal, and lumbar vertebrae, and the sacrum and coccyx. Bony processes and the shape of the vertebrae create openings on both sides through which pass spinal nerves to the neck, trunk, and upper and lower extremities, (Fig. VI-A, b).

THE SYMPATHETIC OR INVOLUNTARY
NERVOUS SYSTEM

This system consists of two main trunks or cords of ganglia (nerve centers), extending from the base of the brain to the coccyx, and situated partly on the right and left sides and partly in front of the spinal column; and, further, of three great nerve plexuses and many smaller ganglia in the body cavities; and of numerous nerve fibers extending from these structures. The two cords converge above in a small ganglion in the brain, and below in the coccygeal ganglion in front of the coccyx.

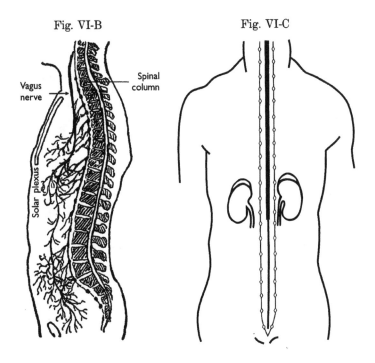

Fig. VI-B   Fig. VI-C

Vagus nerve

Spinal column

Solar plexus

In Fig. VI-B, to the left of the spinal column, is indicated one of the two cords of the involuntary nervous system. From it are seen to extend widespread ramifications of nerve fibers, which form the plexuses that are spread like spider webs over the digestive and the other organs in the body cavities; in the solar plexus they are joined by the vagus nerve of the voluntary system.

Fig. VI-C is a sketch indicating the two ganglionic cords of the involuntary system, converging below; running down between them is the spinal cord, terminating near the coccyx. On the sides are indicated the kidneys, topped by the adrenals.

DEFINITIONS AND EXPLANATIONS

The following is an abbreviated list from the Definitions and Explanations section of Thinking and Destiny. *For a better understanding of these terms, the entire book can be accessed at thewordfoundation.org.—Ed.*

Aia: is the name here given to a unit that has successively progressed through each and every degree in being conscious as its function in a University of Laws, in a perfect, sexless and immortal body; which has graduated from nature, and is on the intelligent-side as a point or line distinguishing it from the nature-side.

Appetite: is the desire to gratify taste and smell with material, in response to the urge of entities of nature to keep matter in circulation.

Art: is skill in the expression of feeling and desire.

Atmosphere: is the mass of diffused matter which radiates from and surrounds any object or thing.

Atmosphere, Physical Human: is the spherical mass of radiant, airy, fluid, and solid units emanating from and kept circulating in four constant streams of units in and through the body by the breath, the active side of the breath-form.

Atmosphere of the Human, Psychic: is the active side of the doer, the psychic part of the Triune Self, the passive side of one portion of which exists in the kidneys and adrenals and the voluntary nerves and the blood of the human body. It surges, pounds, pulls and pushes through the blood and nerves of the body in response to the desire and feeling of the doer which re-exists in the body.

Atmosphere of the Human, Mental: is that part of the mental atmosphere of the Triune Self which is through the psychic atmosphere and by means of which the feeling-mind and desire-mind may think at the neutral points between the uninterrupted inflow and outflow of breathing.

Atmosphere, of One's Triune Self, Noetic: is, so to say, the reservoir, from which the Conscious Light is conveyed by the mental and psychic atmospheres to the doer-in-the-body through the breath.

Breath: is the life of the blood, the pervader and builder of tissue, the preserver and destroyer, by or in which all operations of the body continue to exist or pass out of existence, until by thinking it is made to regenerate and restore the body to everlasting life.

Breath-form: is a nature unit which is the individual living form (soul) of each human body. Its breath builds and renews and gives life to tissue according to the pattern furnished by the form, and its form keeps in form the structure, its body, during its presence in the body. Death is the result of its separation from the body.

Cell, A: is an organization composed of transient units of matter from the radiant, airy, fluid, and solid streams of matter, organized into living structure by the related and reciprocal action of four compositor units: the breath-link, life-link, form-link, and cell-link compositor units constituting that cell, which is not visible, not the body of composed transient units which may be visible or seen under a microscope. The four compositor units are linked together and remain in that cell; the transient units are like flowing streams from which the compositors continue to catch and compose transient units into and as the body of that cell during the continuance of the larger organization of which that cell is a component part. The four compositor units of a cell in a human body are indestructible; when they are not supplied with transient units the cell body will cease, be decomposed and disappear, but the compositors of the cell will again build out a body at some future time.

Character: is the degree of honesty and truthfulness of one's feelings and desires, as expressed by his individual thought, word and action. Honesty and truthfulness in thought and act are the fundamentals of good character, the distinguishing marks of a strong and considerate and fearless character. Character is inborn, inherited from one's own former lives, as the predisposition to think and act; it is continued or changed as one chooses.

Conscience: is the sum of knowledge about what should not be done in relation to any moral subject. It is one's standard for right thinking, right feeling, and right action; it is the sound-less voice of rightness in the heart that forbids any thought or act which varies from what it knows to be right. The "No" or "Don't" is the voice of the doer's knowledge concerning what he should avoid or not do or not give consent to be done in any situation.

Consciousness: is the Presence in all things—by which each thing is conscious in the degree in which it is conscious *as* what or *of* what it is or does. As a word it is the adjective "conscious" developed into a noun by the suffix "ness." It is a word unique in language; it has no synonyms, and its meaning extends beyond human comprehension. Consciousness is beginningless, and end-less; it is indivisible, without parts, qualities, states, attributes or limitations. Yet, everything, from the least to the greatest, in and beyond time and space is dependent on it, to be and to do. Its presence in every unit of nature and beyond nature enables all things and beings to be conscious *as* what or *of* what they are, and are to do, to be aware and conscious of all other things and beings, and to progress in continuing higher degrees of being conscious towards the only one ultimate Reality—Consciousness.

Death: is the departure of the conscious self in the body from its fleshly residence, the snapping or severance of the fine elastic silvery thread that connects the breath-form with the body. The severance is caused by the willing or with the consent of oneself to have its body die. With the breaking of the thread, resuscitation is impossible.

Desire: is conscious power within; it brings about changes in itself and causes change in other things. Desire is the active side of the doer-in-the-body, the passive side of which is feeling; but desire cannot act without its other inseparable side, feeling. Desire is indivisible but appears to be divided; it is to be distinguished as: the desire for knowledge and the desire for sex. It is, with feeling, the cause of the production and reproduction of all things known or sensed by the human. As the desire for sex it remains obscure, but manifests through its four branches: the desire for food, the desire for possessions, the desire for a name, and the desire for power, and their innumerable offshoots, such as hunger, love, hate, affection, cruelty, strife, greed, ambition, adventure, discovery, and accomplishment. The desire for knowledge will not be changed; it is constant as the desire for Self-knowledge.

Destiny: is necessity; that which must be or happen, as the result of what has been thought and said or done.

Destiny, Physical: includes everything concerning the heredity and constitution of the human physical body; the senses, sex, form, and features; the health, position in life, family, and human relations; the span of life and manner of death. The body and all concerning the body is the budget of credit and debit which has come over from one's past lives as the result of what one thought and did in those lives, and with which one has to deal in the present life. One cannot escape what the body is and represents. One must accept that and continue to act as in the past, or one may change that past into what one thinks and wills to be, to do, and to have.

Destiny, Psychic: is all that has to do with feeling-and-desire as one's conscious self in the body; it is the result of what in the past one has desired and thought and done, and of that which in the future will result from what one now desires and thinks and does and which will affect one's feeling-and-desire.

Destiny, Mental: is determined as what, of what, and for what the desire and feeling of the doer-in-the-body think. Three minds— the body-mind, desire-mind, and feeling-mind—are put at the service of the doer, by the thinker of its Triune Self. The thinking which the doer does with these three minds is its mental destiny. Its mental destiny is in its mental atmosphere and includes its mental character, mental attitudes, intellectual attainments and other mental endowments.

Destiny, Noetic: is the amount or degree of Self-knowledge that one has of oneself as feeling and desire, which is available, is in that part of the noetic atmosphere which is in one's psychic atmosphere. This is the result of one's thinking and use of one's creative and generative force; it manifests as one's knowledge of humanity and human relations on the one hand, and on the other through physical destiny, as troubles, afflictions, diseases, or infirmities. Self-knowledge is shown by self-control, the control of one's feelings and desires. One's noetic destiny may be seen in time of crisis, when one knows just what should be done for oneself and others. It may also come as intuition for enlightenment on a subject.

Dimensions: are of matter, not of space; space has no dimensions, space is not dimensional. Dimensions are of units; units are indivisible constituents of mass matter; so that matter is a make-up, composed of or as indivisible units related to and distinguished from each other by their particular kinds of matter, as dimensions. Matter is of four dimensions: on-ness, or surface matter; in-ness, or angle matter; throughness, or line matter; and presence, or point matter. The numbering is from the apparent and familiar to the remote.

The first dimension of the units, on-ness or surface units, has no perceptible depth or thickness or solidity; it depends on and particularly needs the second and third dimensions to make it visible, tangible, solid.

The second dimension of the units is in-ness or angle matter; it depends on the third dimension for it to compact surfaces onto surfaces as mass.

The third dimension of the units is throughness or line matter; it depends on the fourth dimension for it to carry, conduct, transmit, transport, import and export matter from the unmanifested non-dimensional matter into in-ness and fix surfaces onto surfaces and so body out and stabilize surfaces as solid surface matter.

The fourth dimension of the units is presence or point matter, a succession of points as the basic matter line of points, along which or through which the next dimension of line matter is built and developed.

Thus it will be seen that unmanifested undimensional matter manifests as or through or by means of a point, and as a succession of points as a matter line of point units, by means of which the next dimension of units as line matter is developed, and by means of which is in-ness or angle matter, which compacts surfaces on surfaces until visible tangible solid matter is shown as the acts, objects and events of this objective physical world.

Disease: A disease results from the cumulative action of a thought as it continues to pass through the part or body to be affected, and eventually the exteriorization of such thought is the disease.

Doer: That conscious and inseparable part of the Triune Self which periodically re-exists in the man body or woman body, and which usually identifies itself as the body and by the name of the body. It is of twelve portions, six of which are its active side as desire and six are its passive side as feeling. The six active portions of desire re-exist successively in man bodies and the six passive portions of feeling re-exist successively in woman bodies. But desire and feeling are never separate; desire in the man body caused the body to be male and dominates its feeling side; and feeling in the woman body caused its body to be female and dominates its desire side.

Duty: is what one owes to oneself or to others, which must be paid, willingly or unwillingly, in such performance as that duty calls for. Duties bind the doer-in-the-body to repeated lives on earth, until the doer frees itself by performance of all duties, willingly and gladly, without hope of praise or fear of blame, and being unattached to the results well done.

Ego: is the feeling of the identity of "I" of the human, due to the relation of feeling to the identity of I-ness of its Triune Self. The ego usually includes the personality of body with itself, but the ego is only the *feeling* of identity. If the feeling were the identity, the feeling in the body would know itself as the permanent and deathless "I" which persists through and beyond all time in unbroken continuity, whereas the human ego knows no more about itself than that it is "a feeling."

Element, An: is one of the four fundamental kinds of nature units into which nature as matter is classified and of which all bodies or phenomena are composed, so that each element may be distinguished by its kind from each of the other three elements, and so that each kind may be known by its character and function, whether combining and acting as forces of nature or in the composition of any body.

Elemental, An: is a unit of nature manifesting as of the element of fire, or of air, or of water, or of earth, individually; or as an individual unit of an element in a mass of other nature units and dominating that mass of units.

Elementals, Lower: are of the four elements of fire, air, water, and earth units, here called causal, portal, form, and structure units. They are the causes, changes, maintainers, and appearances of all things in nature which come into existence, which change, which remain for awhile, and which will dissolve and vanish, to be re-created into other appearances.

Elementals, Upper: are beings of the fire, air, water, and earth elements, out of which they are created by Intelligences of the spheres, or by the Triune Selves complete, who constitute The Government of the world. Of themselves these beings know nothing and can do nothing. They are not individual nature elementals as nature units, in process of development. They are created out of the unmanifested side of the elements by thinking, and respond perfectly to the thinking of the Triune Selves who direct them in what they are to do. They are executioners of law, against which no nature gods or other forces can prevail. In religions or traditions they may be mentioned as archangels, angels, or messengers. They act by direct order of The Government of the world, without human instrumentality, although one or more may appear to give instruction to the human, or to bring about changes in the affairs of men.

Emotion: is the rousing and expression of desire by words or acts, in response to sensations of pain or pleasure by feeling.

Eternal, The: is that which is unaffected by time, the beginningless and endless, within and beyond time and the senses, not dependent on, limited or measurable by time and the senses as past, present, or future; that in which things are known to be as they are, and which cannot appear to be as they are not.

Facts: are the realities of the objective or subjective acts, objects or events in the state or on the plane on which they are experienced or observed, as evident to and tried by the senses, or as considered and judged by reason. Facts are of four kinds: physical facts, psychic facts, mental facts, and noetic facts.

Faith: is the imagination of the doer which makes a strong impression on the breath-form because of trust and confidence without doubt. Faith comes from the doer.

Fear: is the feeling of foreboding or impending danger concerning mental or emotional or physical trouble.

Feeling: is that of one's conscious self in the body which feels; which feels the body, but does not identify and distinguish itself as feeling, from the body and the sensations which it feels; it is the passive side of the doer-in-the-body, the active side of which is desire.

Food: is of nature material composed of innumerable combinations of compounds of fire, air, water, and earth units, for the building up of the four systems and the upkeep of the body.

Form: is the idea, type, pattern or design which guides and shapes and sets bounds to life as growth; and form holds and fashions structure into visibility as appearance.

Function: is the course of action intended for a person or thing, and which is performed by choice, or by necessity.

God, A: is a thought being, created by the thoughts of human beings as the representative of the greatness of what they feel or fear; as what any one would or might like to be, to will, and to do.

Government, Self-: Self, oneself, is the sum of the feelings and desires of the conscious doer who is within the human body and who is the operator of the body. Government is authority, administration and method by which a body or state is ruled. Self-government means that one's feelings and desires which are or may be inclined, through preferences, prejudices or passions to disrupt the body, will be restrained and guided and governed by one's own better feelings and desires which think and act with rightness and reason, as the standards of authority from within, instead of being controlled by the likes and dislikes concerning the objects of the senses, which are the authorities from outside the body.

Grace: is loving kindness in behalf of others, and ease of thought and feeling expressed in conscious relation to form and action.

Habit: is the expression by word or act of an impression on the breath-form by thinking. Repetition of strange sounds or acts often causes uneasiness of the individual and of the observer, which is likely to become increasingly more pronounced unless the cause is removed. This can be done by not continuing the thinking which causes the habit, or by positive thinking to: "stop" and "do not repeat"—whatever the word or act is. The positive thinking and mental attitude against the habit will efface the impression on the breath-form, and so prevent its recurrence.

Hearing: is the unit of air, acting as the ambassador of the air element of nature in a human body. Hearing is the channel through which the air element of nature and the respiratory system in the body communicate with each other. Hearing is the nature unit which passes through and relates and vitalizes the organs of the respiratory system, and functions as hearing through the right relation of its organs.

DEFINITIONS AND EXPLANATIONS

Heaven: is the state and period of happiness, not limited by the earthly time of the senses, and which seems to have no beginning. It is a composite of all one's thoughts and ideals of life on earth, where no thought of suffering or unhappiness can enter, because these as memories were removed from the breath-form during the purgatorial period. Heaven really begins when the doer is ready and takes on its breath-form. This does not seem like a beginning; it is as though it had always been. Heaven ends when the doer has gone through and exhausted the good thoughts and good deeds which it had and did while on earth. Then the senses of sight and hearing and taste and smell are loosened from the breath-form, and go into the elements of which they were the expression in the body; the portion of the doer returns into itself, istence, where it is until its turn comes for its next re-existence on earth.

Hell: is an individual condition or state of suffering, of torment, not a community affair. The suffering or torment is by parts of the feelings and desires which have been separated from and sloughed off by the doer in its passage through metempsychosis. The suffering is because the feelings and desires have no means by or through which they can be relieved, or of getting what they grieve for, crave and desire. That is their torment—hell. While in a physical body on earth, the good and evil feelings and desires had their periods of joy and sorrow which were intermingled throughout that life on earth. But during metempsychosis, the purgatorial process separates the evil from the good; the good go on to enjoy their unalloyed happiness in "heaven," and the evil remain in what then is torment of suffering, where the individual feelings and desires can be and are impressed, so that when they are again brought together, they can, if they choose, shun the evil and profit from the good. Heaven and hell are for experiencing, but not for learning. Earth is the place for learning from experience, because earth is the place for thinking and learning. In the states after death the thoughts and deeds are as in a dream lived over again, but there is no reasoning or new thinking.

Honesty: is the desire to think of and see things as the Conscious Light in thinking shows these things as they really are and then to deal with those things as the Conscious Light shows that they should be dealt with.

Human Being, A: is a composition of units of the four elements of nature composed and organized as cells and organs into four systems represented by the four senses of sight, hearing, taste, and smell, and automatically coordinated and operated by the

57

breath-form, the general manager of the man body or woman body; and, into which a portion of the doer enters and re-exists, and makes the animal human.

Humanity: is the common origin and relation of all the incorporeal and immortal doers in human bodies, and is the sympathetic feeling in human beings of that relation.

Identity, One's: is the feeling of identity in one's body, one's own feeling as being the same now as what one was in the past, and the same feeling to be in the future. One's feeling of identity is necessary and certain in the doer through the body, because of its inseparability from the identity of the knower of one's Triune Self.

I-ness: is the incorporeal, undying, and continuously unchanging identity of the Triune Self in the Eternal; not embodied, but whose presence enables feeling in the human body to think and feel and speak of itself as "I" and to be conscious of the unchanging identity throughout the constantly changing life of its corporeal body.

Ignorance: is mental darkness, the state in which the doer-in-the-body is, without knowledge of itself and of its rightness and reason. The emotions and passions of its feeling and desire have eclipsed its thinker and knower. Without the Conscious Light from them it is in darkness. It cannot distinguish itself from the senses and the body it is in.

Intelligence, An: is of the highest order of units in the Universe, relating the Triune Self of man with the Supreme Intelligence through its self-conscious Light, with which it endows man and so enables him to think.

Intelligence, Faculties of an: There are seven: the light and I-am faculties which govern the sphere of fire; the time and motive faculties governing the sphere of air; the image and dark faculties in the sphere of water; and the focus faculty in the sphere of earth. Each faculty has its own particular function and power and purpose and is inseparably interrelated with the others. The light faculty sends light to the worlds by means of its Triune Self; the time faculty is that which causes the regulation and changes in nature units in their relation to each other. The image faculty impresses the idea of form on matter. The focus faculty centers other faculties on the subject to which it is directed. The

DEFINITIONS AND EXPLANATIONS

dark faculty resists or gives strength to the other faculties. The motive faculty gives purpose and direction to thought. The I-am faculty is the real Self of the Intelligence. The focus faculty is the only one which comes into contact with the body through the doer in the body.

Intelligence, The Supreme: is the limit and ultimate degree that an intelligent unit can advance to in being conscious as a unit. The Supreme Intelligence represents and comprehends all other Intelligences in the spheres. It is not the ruler of other Intelligences, because Intelligences know all law; they are law and each Intelligence rules itself and thinks and acts in accord with universal law. But the Supreme Intelligence has in its charge and supervision all the spheres and worlds and knows the gods and beings throughout universal nature.

Justice: is the action of knowledge in relation to the subject under consideration, and in judgment pronounced and prescribed as law.

Knower, The: is that of the Triune Self which has and is actual and real knowledge, of and in time and the Eternal.

Knowledge is of Two Kinds: real or Self-knowledge and sense- or human knowledge. Self-knowledge of the Triune Self is inexhaustible and immeasurable and is common to the knowers of all Triune Selves. It is not dependent on the senses though it includes all that has taken place in the worlds; this concerns everything from the least developed unit of nature to the all-knowing Triune Self of the worlds throughout the entirety of time in the Eternal. It is the real and unchanging knowledge at once available in the minutest detail and as one perfectly related and complete whole.

Sense-knowledge, science, or human knowledge, is the accumulated and systematized sum of the facts of nature observed as natural laws, or experienced by the doers through their undeveloped senses and imperfect bodies. And the knowledge and statements of the laws have to be changed from time to time.

Life: is a unit of growth, the carrier of light through form. Life acts as agent between the above and the below, bringing the fine into the gross and reconstructing and transforming the gross into refinement. In every seed there is a unit of life. In man it is the breath-form.

Life (To One's Critical Understanding): is more or less of a nightmare, an apparently real but uncertain series of sudden or long drawn out, more or less vivid and intense happenings—a phantasmagoria.

Light: is that which makes things visible, but which cannot itself be seen. It is composed of the units of starlight or sunlight or moonlight or earthlight, or of the combination or condensation and expression of these as electricity or as the combustion of gases, fluids or solids.

Light, Attachable and Unattachable: is the Conscious Light of the Intelligence loaned to the Triune Self, which the doer-in-the-body uses in its thinking. The attachable light is that which the doer sends into nature by its thoughts and acts, and reclaims and uses again and again. The unattachable Light is that which the doer has reclaimed and made unattachable, because it has balanced the thoughts in which the Light was. Light that is made unattachable is restored to one's noetic atmosphere and is available to that one as knowledge.

Light, Conscious: is the Light which the Triune Self receives from its Intelligence. It is not nature nor reflected by nature, though, when it is sent into nature and associates with nature units, nature seems to manifest intelligence, and it may be called the God in nature. When, by thinking, the Conscious Light is turned and held on any thing, it shows that thing to be as it is. The Conscious Light is therefore Truth, because Truth shows things to be as they are, without preference or prejudice, without disguise or pretense. All things are made known by it when it is turned and held on them. But the Conscious Light is fogged and obscured by thoughts when feeling-and-desire try to think, so the human being sees things as it wants to see them, or in a modified degree of Truth.

Light in the Doer, Potential: When one performs duties uncomplainingly, ungrudgingly and with pleasure because they are his duties, and not because he will profit or gain or get rid of them, he is balancing his thoughts which made those duties *his* duties, and the Light that he frees when the thoughts are balanced gives him a new sense of the joy of freedom. It gives him an insight into things and subjects he had not understood before. As he continues to free the Light he had kept bound in the things he craved and wanted, he begins to feel and understand the potential Light that is in him and which will be actual Conscious Light when he becomes an Intelligence.

DEFINITIONS AND EXPLANATIONS

Light of Nature: is the reaction as shine, sparkle, brightness or glitter of combinations of nature units, to the Conscious Light sent into nature by the doers in human bodies.

Matter: is substance manifested as unintelligent units as nature, and, which progress to be intelligent units as Triune Selves.

Meaning: is the intention in a thought expressed.

Mind: is the functioning of intelligent-matter. There are seven minds, that is, seven kinds of thinking by the Triune Self, with the Light of the Intelligence,—yet they are one. All seven kinds are to act according to one principle, which is, to hold the Light steadily on the subject of the thinking. They are: the mind of I-ness and the mind of selfness of the knower; the mind of rightness and the mind of reason of the thinker; the mind of feeling and the mind of desire of the doer; and the body-mind which is also used by the doer for nature, and for nature only.

The term "mind" is here used as that function or process or thing with which or by which thinking is done. It is a general term here for the seven minds, and each of the seven is of the reason side of the thinker of the Triune Self. Thinking is the steady holding of the Conscious Light on the subject of the thinking. The mind for I-ness and the mind for selfness are used by the two sides of the knower of the Triune Self. The mind for rightness and the mind of reason are used by the thinker of the Triune Self. The feeling-mind and the desire-mind and body-mind are to be used by the doer: the first two to distinguish feeling and desire from the body and nature and to have them in balanced union; the body-mind is to be used through the four senses, for the body and its relation to nature.

Mind, The Body-: The real purpose of the body-mind is for the use of feeling-and-desire, to care for and to control the body, and through the body to guide and control the four worlds by means of the four senses and their organs in the body. The body-mind can think only through the senses and in terms restricted to the senses and sensuous matter. Instead of being controlled, the body-mind controls feeling-and-desire so that they are unable to distinguish themselves from the body, and the body-mind so dominates their thinking that they are compelled to think in terms of the senses instead of in terms suited to feeling-and-desire.

Mind, The Feeling-: is that with which feeling thinks, according to its four functions. These are perceptiveness, conceptiveness,

61

formativeness, and projectiveness. But instead of using these for the emancipation of itself from bondage to nature, they are controlled through the body-mind by nature through the four senses: sight, hearing, taste, and smell.

Mind, The Desire-: which desire should use to discipline and control feeling and itself; to distinguish itself as desire from the body in which it is; and, to bring about the union of itself with feeling; it has, instead, allowed itself to be subordinate to and to be controlled by the body-mind in service to the senses and to objects of nature.

Morals: are determined to the degree that one's feelings and desires are guided by the soundless voice of conscience in the heart concerning what not to do, and by the sound judgment of reason, as to what to do. Then, notwithstanding allurements of the senses, one's conduct will be straightforward and right, with respect to oneself and with consideration for others. One's morals will be the background of one's mental attitude.

Nature: is a machine composed of the totality of unintelligent units; units that are conscious as their functions only.

Noetic: That which is of knowledge or related to knowledge.

Number: is One, a whole, as a circle, in which all numbers are included.

Numbers: are the principles of being, in continuity and relation to unity, Oneness.

One: is a unit, a unity or whole, the origin and inclusion of all numbers as its parts, in extension or completion.

Passion: is the raging of feelings and desires concerning objects or subjects of the senses.

Patience: is calm and careful persistence in the accomplishment of desire or purpose.

Perfect Physical Body: is the state or condition which is the ultimate, the complete; from which nothing can be lost, nor to which anything can be added. Such is the perfect sexless physical body of the Triune Self in the Realm of Permanence.

DEFINITIONS AND EXPLANATIONS

Personality: is the corporeal human body, the mask, in and through which the incorporeal doer of desire-and-feeling thinks and speaks and acts.

Plan: is that which shows the way or the means by which purpose is accomplished.

Power, Conscious: is desire, which brings about changes in itself, or which causes change in other things.

Prejudice: is judging a person, place or thing to which feeling-and-desire are opposed, without considering, or regardless of, right or reason. Prejudice prevents right and just judgment.

Principle, A: is that fundamental in a thing of which it was, by which it came to be what it is, and according to which its character may be known wherever it is.

Purpose: is the guiding motive in effort as the immediate thing, for which one strives, or the ultimate subject to be known; it is the conscious direction of force, the intention in words or in action, the accomplishment of thought and effort, the end of attainment.

Realm of Permanence, The: pervades the phantasmagoria of this human world of birth and death, like as sunlight pervades the air we breathe. But the mortal sees and understands the Realm no more than we see or understand the sunlight. The reason is that the senses and perceptions are unbalanced, and not attuned to things that time and death cannot affect. But the Realm of Permanence bears up and preserves the human world from utter destruction, as sunlight does the life and growth of living things. The conscious doer in the body will understand and perceive the Realm of Permanence as he understands and distinguishes himself from the changing body in which he desires and feels and thinks.

Reason: is the analyzer, regulator and judge; the administrator of justice as the action of knowledge according to the law of rightness. It is the answer of questions and problems, the beginning and the end of thinking, and the guide to knowledge.

Re-Existence: is the doer portion leaving the other portions of itself, in istence, to re-exist away from itself, in nature, when the animal human body has been prepared and made ready for it to enter and take a life residence in that body. The animal body is made ready by training it to make use of its senses, to walk, and to repeat the words which it is trained to use. That it does, like a parrot, while it is still animal. It becomes human as soon as it is intelligent, as shown by questions that it asks, and what it understands.

Relation: is the origin and sequence in ultimate unity by which all nature units and intelligent units and Intelligences are related in Conscious Sameness.

Resurrection: has a twofold meaning. The first is the gathering together of the four senses and the compositors of the body of the past life, which were distributed into nature after its death, and the rebuilding by the breath-form of a new fleshly body to serve as the residence of the doer on its return to earth life. The second and real meaning is that the doer in the man or woman body regenerates the sexual body from the imperfect man or woman body that is, to a body where the essentials of the two sexes are merged into one perfect physical body and restored, resurrected, to its former and original and immortal state of perfection.

Right: is the sum of knowledge of which one is conscious, as his rule of action from within.

Rightness: is the standard of thinking and action, as the law prescribed and the rule of conduct, for the doer of feeling-and-desire in the body. It is located in the heart.

Selfness: is knowledge of itself as the knower of the Triune Self.

Senses of the Body: are the ambassadors of nature at the court of man; the representatives of the four great elements of fire, air, water, and earth, which are individualized as sight, hearing, taste, and smell of the human body.

Sexes: are the exteriorizations in nature of the thoughts of desire and feeling resulting in male and female bodies.

Sight: is a unit of fire, acting as the ambassador of the fire element of nature in the body of man. Sight is the channel through which the fire element of nature and the generative system in the body act and react on each other. Sight is the nature unit which

64

relates and coordinates the organs of the generative system and functions as sight by the proper relation of its organs.

Sin: is the thinking and doing what one knows to be wrong, against rightness, what one knows to be right. Any departure from what one knows to be right, is sin. There are sins against oneself, against others, and against nature. The penalties of sin are pain, disease, suffering, and, eventually, death. The original sin is the thought, followed by the sexual act.

Skill: is the degree of art in the expression of what one thinks and desires and feels.

Smell: is a unit of the earth element, the representative of the earth element in a human body. Smell is the ground on which the earth element of nature and the digestive system in the body meet and contact. Sight acts with hearing, hearing acts through taste, taste acts in smell, smell acts on the body. Sight is the fiery, hearing the airy, taste the watery, and smell the solid earthy. Smell is the basis on which the other three senses act.

Soul: The indefinite something of religions and philosophies, sometimes said to be immortal and at other times said to be subject to death, whose origin and destiny have been variously accounted for, but which has always been said to be a part of or associated with the human body. It is the form or passive side of the breath-form of every human body; its active side is the breath.

Spirit: is the active side of a nature unit which energizes and operates through the other or passive side of itself, called matter.

Substance: is boundless space, without parts, homogeneous, the same throughout, the all containing "no thing," unconscious sameness, which is, nevertheless, present throughout nature.

Symbol, A: is a visible object to represent an invisible subject which one is to think of, as itself or in relation to another subject.

Taste: is a unit of the water element of nature progressed to the degree of acting as a minister of nature in the human body. Taste is the channel in which the water element of nature and the circulatory system in the body circulate in each other. Taste is the nature unit which commingles and relates the units of air and earth in its units of water to prepare them for circulation and digestion and in its own organs to function as taste.

Thinker: The real thinker of the Triune Self is between its knower, and its doer in the human body. It thinks with the mind of rightness and the mind of reason. There is no hesitancy or doubt in its thinking, no disagreement between its rightness and reason. It makes no mistakes in its thinking; and what it thinks is at once effective.

The doer-in-the-body is spasmodic and unsteady in thinking; its feeling-and-desire-minds are not always in agreement, and their thinking is controlled by the body-mind that thinks through the senses and of the objects of the senses. And, instead of with the clear Light, the thinking is done usually in a fog and with the Light diffused in the fog. Yet, the civilization in the world is the result of the thinking and the thoughts that have made it. Were some of the doers in human bodies to become conscious that they are the immortals that they are, and to control instead of being controlled by, their body-minds, they could then turn the earth into a garden in every way superior to the legendary paradise.

Thinking: is the steady holding of the Conscious Light within on the subject of the thinking. It is a process of (1) the selection of a subject or the formulation of a question; (2) turning the Conscious Light on it, which is done by giving one's undivided attention to it; (3) by the steady holding and focusing the Conscious Light on the subject or question; and (4) by bringing the Light to a focus on the subject as a point. When the Conscious Light is focused on the point, the point opens into fullness of the entire knowledge of the subject selected or in answer to the question formulated. Thinking affects subjects according to their susceptibility and by the rightness and the power of the thinking.

Thinking, Active: is the intention to think on a subject, and is the effort to hold the Conscious Light within on the subject, until that subject is known, or until the thinking is distracted or turned to another subject.

Thinking, Passive: is the thinking that is done without any definite intent; it is started by a fleeting thought or an impression of the senses; the idle play or day-dreaming involving one or all three minds of the doer in such Light as may be in the psychic atmosphere.

DEFINITIONS AND EXPLANATIONS

Thinking That Does Not Create Thoughts, That Is, Destiny: Why does a person think? He thinks because his senses compel him to think, about objects of the senses, about persons and events, and his reactions to them. And when he thinks he wants to be something, to do something, or to get or to have something. *He wants!* And when he wants he attaches himself and the Light in a thought, to what he wants; he has created a thought. That means that the Light in his thinking is welded with his desire that wants, to the matter and course of action, or to the object or thing he wants. By that thought he has attached and bound the Light and himself. And the only way he can ever free the Light and himself from that bond is to be unattached; that is, he must balance the thought which binds him, by freeing the Light and his desire from the thing it *wants*. To do this, it usually takes countless lives, ages, to learn, to understand; to understand that he cannot act as well and as freely with the thing to which he is attached and bound, as he can if he were not attached, not bound. Your desire is *you!* The action or thing you want is not you. If you attach and bind yourself to it by a thought, you cannot act as well as if you are unbound and free to act without attachment. Therefore, the thinking that does not create thoughts is in being free to think, and to not want, have, hold, but to act, to have, to hold, without being bound to the act, to what you have, to what you hold. That is, to think in freedom. Then you can think clearly, with clear Light, and with power.

Thought, A: is a living being in nature, conceived and gestated in the heart by feeling-and-desire with the Conscious Light, elaborated in and issued from the brain, and which will exteriorize as an act, object or event, again and again, until it is balanced. The parent doer of the thought is responsible for all results that flow from it until that thought is balanced; that is, by the experiences from the exteriorizations, the learning from experiences, the doer frees the Light and the feeling-and-desire from the object of nature to which they were bound, and so acquires knowledge.

Thought, Balancing a: Thinking extracts the Light from a thought when feeling-and-desire are in agreement with each other and both are in agreement with selfness concerning the act, object or event which has been witnessed by I-ness. Then the thinking transfers and restores the Light to the noetic atmosphere and the thought is balanced, ceases to exist.

Thought, The Balancing Factor in a: is the mark which conscience stamps on a thought as its seal of disapproval at the time of the creation of the thought by feeling and desire. Through all the changes and exteriorizations of the thought, the mark remains until the balancing of that thought. The mark and the thought disappear when the thought is balanced.

Thought, Ruling: One's presiding thought at the time of death is the ruling thought for the following life on earth. It may be changed, but while it rules it influences his thinking, helps in the selection of his associates and leads or introduces him to others of similar thought. It often decides in the selection of a profession or business or occupation which he may follow through life. While it remains his ruling thought it tempers his disposition and gives color to his outlook on life.

Thoughts, Visiting: Thoughts circulate; they are as gregarious as their parents are; they visit each other in the mental atmospheres of human beings, because of the aims and objects for which they are created, and they meet in the atmosphere of the similar interests of the human beings who create them. Thoughts are the chief causes of the meeting and association of people; the likeness of their thoughts draw people together.

Time: is the change of units or of masses of units in their relation to each other. There are many kinds of time in the worlds and in the different states. For example: the mass of units composing the sun, the moon, the earth, changing in their relation to each other, are measured as sun time, moon time, earth time.

Triune Self: The indivisible self-knowing and immortal One; its identity and knowledge part as knower; its rightness and reason part as thinker, in the Eternal; and, its desire and feeling part as doer, existing periodically on the earth.

Trust: is the fundamental belief in the honesty and truthfulness of other human beings, because there is the deep seated honesty in the one who trusts. When one is disappointed by his misplaced trust in another, he should not lose trust in himself, but he should learn to be careful, careful of what and in whom he trusts.

Types: A type is the initial or beginning of form, and the form is the inclusion and completion of the type. Thoughts are the types of the animals and objects and are forms bodied out as the expressions of human feelings and desires on the screen of nature.

DEFINITIONS AND EXPLANATIONS

Understanding: is the perceiving and feeling what things are of themselves, what their relations are, and comprehending why they are so and are so related.

Unit, A: is an indivisible and irreducible one, a circle, which has an unmanifested side, as shown by a horizontal diameter. The manifested side has an active and a passive side, as shown by a mid-vertical line. Changes made by their interaction are effected by the presence of the unmanifested through both. Every unit has the potentiality of becoming one with the ultimate reality—Consciousness—by its constant progression in being conscious in ever higher degrees.

Units, Nature: are distinguished by being conscious *as* their functions only. Nature units are not conscious *of* anything. There are four kinds: free units which are unbound and unattached to other units in mass or structure; transient units, which are composed into or cohere in structure or mass for a time and then pass on; compositor units, which compose and hold transient units for a time; and sense units, as sight, hearing, taste, and smell, which control or govern the four systems of the human body. All nature units are unintelligent.

Virtue: is power, strength of will, in the practice of honesty and truthfulness.

Will, Free: Will is the dominant desire, of the moment, of a period, or of the life. It dominates its opposing desires and may dominate the desires of others. Desire is the conscious power within, which may bring about changes in itself or which changes other things. No desire in the human is free, because it is attached or attaches itself to objects of the senses when thinking. One desire may control or be controlled by another desire, but no desire can change another desire or be compelled to change itself. No power other than its own can change it. A desire may be subdued, crushed, and made subordinate, but it cannot be made to change itself unless it chooses and wills to change. It is free to choose whether it will or will not change itself. This power to choose whether it will remain attached to this or that thing, or whether it will let go of the thing and be unattached, is its point of freedom, the point of freedom that every desire is and has. It may extend its point to an area of freedom by willing to be, to do, or to have, without attaching itself to what it wills to be, to do, or to have. When the will thinks without being attached to what it thinks, it is free, and has freedom. In freedom, it can be

69

or do or have what it wills to be or do or have, as long as it remains unattached. Free will is to be unattached, unattachment.

Wisdom: is the right use of knowledge.

Work: is mental or bodily activity, the means and the manner by which purpose is accomplished.

INDEX

A

Adrenals, 15, 48
  third step, 15
Aia, 25
  definition, 49
AOM, *See* IAOM
Appetite, 11
  definition, 49
Apprentice. *See* Entered Apprentice
Apron, the, 9, 11, 15, 18, 38
Ark of the Covenant, 34
Art, 15
  definition, 49
Ashler, the
  rough and perfect, 10, 11
Assaults, the three, 22
Atmosphere(s)
  definition, 49
  mental, 31, 49
  noetic, 31, 50
  physical, 49
  psychic, 31, 49

B

Boaz and Jachin, 28, 33
  bridge, building the, 14, 26
  columns or pillars and, 26
  meaning of, 14
  thinker and knower, 38
  union of, 33
Body, human physical, 43
  brain, 20, 21, 47, 48
  coccygeal ganglion/gland, 28, 48
  is potentially a complete universe, 24
  new parts, organs, channels in the, 21
  organs in the, 14, 21
  preserving the, 9
  ruins of Solomon's Temple, 2, 15, 22
  spine, 21, 25, 28, 29, 33, 47, 48

  sympathetic/involuntary nervous
    system, 14, 20, 21, 48
  the broken column, 25, 44
  the three, five and seven
    steps in the, 14
  Zodiac and the, 23
  See also Adrenals; Kidneys;
    Lodge, the; Pineal body;
    Pituitary body
Body, immortal, 21, 26, 30, 34, 37, 43
  perfect physical body, 2, 11, 36, 62
  plan of is within Hiram Abiff, 26
  the Word and, 35
Body-mind. *See* Mind(s)
Brain. *See* Body, human physical
Breath
  definition, 50
Breath-form
  definition, 50
  lines on the, 4, 7, 11, 21, 25, 29
  See also Soul
Bridge. *See* Boaz and Jachin

C

Cable-tow, the, 18, 38
  meaning of, 7
  rebirth and, 21
  senses and, 7, 31
  umbilical cord, 7
Candidate, the
  conscious self in the body, 7
  doer, the, 15, 31
  feeling-and-desire, 37
  Hiram Abiff, 20
  is raised, 26
  prerequisites, 6
Cell, a, 17
  definition, 50
Ceremonies
  purpose of, 12, 33

Chamber, the Middle. *See* Middle
Chamber of King Solomon's Temple
Character, 1, 6, 24, 40
definition, 50
Circle, the
squaring, 44, 45
symbol of the Word, 36
twelve nameless points of, 17, 40
See also Point and the Circle, the;
Zodiac, the
Columns or pillars, the, 14, 26, 33,
38, 43
Beauty, the doer/Hiram Abiff, 26, 38
spinal/Jachin, 14, 26
Strength, the thinker/Hiram,
King of Tyre, 26, 38
sympathetic /nature/
Boaz, 14, 26, 28, 48
the broken, 25, 44
Wisdom, the knower/King
Solomon, 26, 38
Compass, the, 7, 16, 31, 36, 38
Conscience
definition, 50
Conscious Light. *See* Light
Consciousness
definition, 51

D

Daily work, the, 30
Death, 2, 25, 37
definition, 51
Degrees, the, 43
Entered Apprentice, 3, 11,
14, 30, 31, 37, 38, 43
Fellow Craft, 3, 13, 18,
30, 31, 37, 38
foundation of Masonry, 30, 37
fourth through seventh, 37–40
Mark Master, 32
Masonry, of, 3, 16
Master Mason, 3, 18,
30, 31, 37, 38, 43
Most Excellent Master, 33
Past Master, 32
principles of the three, 3
Royal Arch, 3, 31, 34, 43, 44, 45
Desire, 15, 38
definition, 51

desires and, 5, 6, 8, 15, 18
sex power carried by, 20
See also Feeling-and-desire
Desire-mind. *See* Mind(s)
Destiny, 5, 7
definition, 52
mental, 52
noetic, 52
physical, 52
psychic, 52
Dimensions
definition, 52
Discipline
feelings and desires, of, 5
minds, of the, 5
Disease, 21
definition, 53
Divestment, the, 6
Doer, the, 26, 37, 43
balancer, the, 38
candidate, the, 15, 31
definition, 53
Entered Apprentice, 8, 11,
18, 30, 37, 38, 43
first came into his body, 14
fundamental teachings of
Masonry and, 38
Hiram Abiff, 22, 25, 38
Jubela, 22, 38
Junior Warden, 21, 29, 38
Lost Word, 22, 36
pillar of Beauty, 38
power, 22, 29
the Word and, 35
Third Logos, 36
See also Desire; Feeling;
Feeling-and-desire
Duty
definition, 54
Senior and Junior Warden's, 29
to rebuild the temple, 37

E

Earth Spirit, 35
Ego, 23
definition, 54
Element, An, 9, 16, 20, 22, 35
definition, 54
Elemental(s), 21, 29, 30

definition, 54
lower, 54
upper, 54
Emotion(s), 21, 23
definition, 55
Entered Apprentice. *See* Degrees, the
Eternal, the
definition, 55
Euclid
47th proposition of, 26

F

Facts, 6
definition, 55
Faith
definition, 55
Fear, 11
definition, 55
Feeling, 15, 38
definition, 55
feelings and, 5, 8, 15, 18
moon and, 8
See also Feeling-and-desire
Feeling-and-desire, 10, 18, 22, 26
symbols and, 38
the Word is, 36
training of, 37
two stewards, 29
See also Desire; Doer, the; Feeling
Feeling-mind. *See* Mind(s)
Fellow Craft. *See* Degrees, the
Food, 9, 25
definition, 55
Form, 4, 39, 40
definition, 56
Fortitude, 11
Freemasons, the Brotherhood of, 1
Function
definition, 56

G

G, 38
meaning of the letter, 16, 17
Gauge, the, 10
Gavel, the, 10
Geometrical symbols. *See* Symbols
Geometry, 15, 16, 17, 21
Germ. *See* Lunar germ; Solar germ

Glory of the Lord fills the Lord's house, the, 31, 33, 34
God(s)
Brahma, Vishnu, Shiva, 35
Christian, 3
conduct towards, 12
definition, 56
Intelligence as, 36
Jehovah, 35
service of, 10
Supreme Intelligence, 24
the letter G and, 16
the Name, the Word and, 34
Triune Self, 7
Word of, 8
Government, Self-, 9
definition, 56
Grace, 2
definition, 56
Great Architect, the, 17
Great Way, the, 40
Great Work, the, 41

H

Habit
definition, 56
Hearing, 7
definition, 56
See also Senses of the body
Heart
fourth step, 15
preparations in the, 6, 11
Sanctum Sanctorum, 21
Heaven
definition, 57
fire coming down from, 34
Hell
definition, 57
Hiram Abiff, 20–27
candidate, 20
doer, the, 22, 25, 38
life, death, resurrection of, 20
meaning of, 20, 22
monument to the memory of, 25
pillar of Beauty, 26
plan of immortal body is within, 26
power that makes the rounds, the, 24
raising of, 25, 26
restrained from going out, 21

slain at the East gate, 24
three burials of, 25
Word, is the, 22
Hiram, King of Tyre
pillar of Strength, 26
thinker, the, 22, 25, 38
Hiram's mark
H.S.W.K. and T.T.S.S., 33
Honesty, 6
definition, 57
Hoodwink, the, 7, 18, 26
Human Being
definition, 57
doer in the, 22
Masonic teachings and the, 2, 4
zodiac and the, 23
Human body. *See* Body, human
Humanity
definition, 58
Entered Apprentice tied to, 7
Masonry is for, 1

I

I
false, 22, 23, 25
IAOM.
meaning of, 35
pronunciation of, 36
symbol for, 36
See also Word, the
Identity, One's
definition, 58
Ignorance
definition, 58
feeling-and-desire, 13
Immortal body. *See* Body, immortal
Ineffable Name, the, 36
I-ness, 15
definition, 58
Senior Deacon, 30
See also Knower, the
Initiation, 6, 11, 13, 20, 33
Inner life
Masonry and, 1, 5
Instructions, 7
Instrument, the sharp, 7
Intelligence(s), 20
behind Masonry, 2

definition, 58
faculties of, 20, 58
Geometer, the, 17
God as, 36
Light of, 20, 31, 34, 36
powers, 22
Intelligence, The Supreme
definition, 59
God, 24
source of all Light, 38
symbol of, 38
teachings of Masonry and, 37

J

Jehovah, 35, 38
Jewels, 16
Master's, the, 34
six, 11
Jubela, Jubelo, and Jubelum, 38
meaning of, 21, 22, 23
Junior Warden. *See* Doer, the; Officers
Justice, 11, 30
definition, 59

K

Keystone
mark of Hiram on the, 33
meaning of the, 31, 44, 45
Kidneys, 15, 48
second step, 15
King Solomon, 20, 23, 24, 25, 26
knower, the, 22, 25, 38
pillar of Wisdom, 26
King Solomon's Temple, 2, 11, 14, 20,
25, 28, 32, 34
See also Middle Chamber of King
Solomon's Temple; Temple
Knower, the, 26, 43
conscious relation with, 37
definition, 59
First Logos, 36
fundamental teachings of
Masonry and, 38
Gnosis, 8
Jachin, 38
Jubelum, 22, 38
King Solomon, 22, 25, 38
Light of lights and, 8

Master Mason, 18, 30, 37, 38
pillar of Wisdom, 38
the Word and, 35
Worshipful Master, 21, 30, 38
See also I-ness; Selfness

Knowledge
dispensing, 33
growing in, 9
is of two kinds, 59
justice and, 11

L

Lambskin, 9, 38
Landmarks, the ancient, 5, 38
Level, the, 11, 13, 15, 18
Liberal arts and sciences, the, 15
Life
definition, 59
inner, 5
inward, 1
life (to one's critical
  understanding), 60
understanding of, 5
Light, 4, 38
attachable and unattachable, 60
become children of, 37
candidate (doer) brought
  to the, 13, 18
Conscious, 20, 31, 36, 37, 39, 60
definition, 60
descends into the candidate, 34
desire for, 6, 7
getting/receiving more, 13,
  16, 18, 30, 31, 33, 37, 39
Hiram Abiff has the, 22
in the doer, potential, 60
Intelligence, of the, 20, 31, 36
Masonic teachings, the center of, 37
Masonry, of, 7
Master dispenses his, 29
nature, of, 61
of lights, 8
power of the, 22
rightness-and-reason, 13
the body lived in the, 37
Lights, the three great and lesser,
7–9, 38
Lodge, the
a Mason's own, 30

meaning of, 28
oblong square, as, 28, 31, 38
symbolizes the human body, 8, 28, 43
Logos, 34, 35, 36
Lunar germ, 20, 29, 33
Lungs
fifth step, 15
Sanctum Sanctorum, 21

M

Mark Master. *See* Degrees, the
Masonic drama, the, 20, 23
Masonic Order
importance of the, 5
Masonic prayer, the, 2, 37
Masonic teachings, 2
have become twisted, 38
summary of the, 37--40
Masonry
age of, 1
foundations of, 30
great lesson of, 20
has in trust certain geometrical
  symbols, 40
meaning of the preliminaries, 6
offshoots of, 4
origins of, 1
permanent forms of, 38
plan of, 2
principles of, 3
purpose and plan of, 2–5, 34
religions and, 2
twisted teachings of, 38
Master Mason. *See* Degrees, the
Master of the Lodge. *See* Officers
Matter, 39–40
definition, 61
four states of, 46
nature- and intelligent-, 16
Meaning, 40
definition, 61
Middle Chamber of King Solomon's
Temple, 14, 15, 28, 44
Mind(s)
body-mind, 9, 12, 15, 23, 39, 61
definition, 61
desire-mind, 9, 12, 15, 18, 39, 62
discipline of the, 5

feeling-mind, 9, 12, 15, 18, 39, 61
  reason, of, 15, 18
  rightness, of, 15, 18
  seven, the, 15
  symbols and the, 12, 15, 18
  three, the, 5, 9, 39
Morals, 26
  definition, 62
Most Excellent Master. *See* Degrees,
  the
Motives
  selfish, 23

N

Name, the, 32, 34--36, 39
  pronunciation of, 36
  See also Ineffable Name,
    the; Word, the
Nature
  definition, 62
  Earth Spirit and, 35
  God as, 36
  human body and, 8
  zodiac and, 24
Noetic
  atmosphere, 31
  definition, 62
Number
  definition, 62
  numbers, 62
  numbers, the twelve, 23
  See also One

O

Oblong square, the, 43, 45
  Lodge, as, 28, 31, 38
Officers, 21, 39
  Junior Deacon, 28
  Junior Warden, 21, 28, 33, 38, 43
  Master of the Lodge, Worshipful
    Master, 7, 17, 21, 26, 28, 32, 38, 43
  Secretary, 28
  Senior Deacon, 28
  Senior Warden, 21, 28, 38, 43
  their stations and duties, 28
  Treasurer, 28
OM, *See* IAOM

One
  definition, 62
  See also Number

P

Passion, 8, 10
  definition, 62
Past Master. *See* Degrees, the
Patience, 11
  definition, 62
Personality
  definition, 63
Pillars, *See* Columns or pillars, the
Pineal body
  seventh step, 15
Pituitary body
  sixth step, 15
Plan
  definition, 63
  immortal body, of the, 26
  of Masonry, 2–5
Pledge, the, 7
Plumb, the, 11, 13, 15, 18
Point and the Circle, the, 16, 17, 38
  purpose of, 16
  See also Circle, the; Zodiac, the
Power(s), 20–25
  body, in the, 25
  conscious, 63
  creative, 10
  elements, of the four, 22
  masculine and feminine, 35
  minds, of the, 15
  nature, 22
  psychic and mental, 16
  rightness, of, 13
  twelve, 24
  Word, of the, 36
  See also Desire; Doer,
    the; Hiram Abiff;
    Intelligence(s); Light;
    Sex; Triune Self, the
Prayer. *See* Masonic prayer, the
Prejudice, 39
  definition, 63
Preliminaries, the
  meaning of, 6
Preparations in the heart and for
  initiation, 6, 11

Principle(s)
  definition, 63
  seminal, 20
  three degrees, of the, 3
Prostate
  first step, 15
Prudence, 11
Purpose.
  definition, 63
  of Masonry, 2–5
  See also Ceremonies; Masonry; Point
    and the circle, the; Symbols

R

Realm of Permanence, the, 41, 45
  definition, 63
Reason.
  definition, 63
  Junior Deacon, 30
  mind of, 15, 18
  the compass and, 8
  See also Rightness-and-reason
Re-existence, 7
  definition, 63
Relation
  definition, 64
Religion(s)
  Masonry and, 1, 2
  See also God(s)
Resurrection, 20
  definition, 64
Right
  action, 11
  definition, 64
  rule of, 10, 15
  thinking, 11
Rightness, 13
  definition, 64
  mind of, 15, 18
  the compass and, 8
  See also Rightness-and-reason
Rightness-and-reason, 13,
  See also Reason; Rightness
Rituals, the
  ritualists and, 2, 37–39
Rosicrucianism, 4
Royal Arch. See Degrees, the
Ruffians, the, 21, 39
  finding of the three, 24

S

Sanctum Sanctorum, 21, 25, 28, 44
Secret language, the, 4
Self-government. See Government,
  Self-
Selfness, 15
  definition, 64
  See also Knower, the
Senior Warden. See Officers; Thinker,
  the
Senses of the body, 9, 29
  cable-tow, the, 7, 31
  definition, 64
  See also Hearing; Sight; Smell; Taste
Sex, 9
  center, 29
  gate of, 21, 24
  power, 20–26, 29, 37
Sexes, the
  definition, 64
  power of, 22
Sharp instrument, the. See Instru-
  ment, the sharp
Sight, 4, 7
  definition, 64
  See also Senses of the body
Signs and their meanings, 10
Signs, grips and words, 4, 9, 10,
  13, 18
Sin, 2, 37
  definition, 65
Skill, 11
  definition, 65
Smell, 7
  definition, 65
Solar germ, 29
Solomon's Temple, King. See King
  Solomon's Temple
Soul, 17
  definition, 65
  See also Breath-form
South gate, the, 21, 23
  gate of sex, 21
Speculative Masonry, 10, 15
Spirit
  definition, 65
  See also Earth Spirit

Square, the, 7, 13, 15, 16, 31, 36, 38, 43
symbolizes desire, 11
Squaring the circle, 44, 45
Star(s), 38
blazing, 11, 38
six pointed, 24, 31
Steps, the 3, 5 and 7, 14
Substance, 16
definition, 65
Royal Arch and, 16
Symbols
definition, 65
for IAOM, the Word, 36
from *Thinking and Destiny*, 46–48
geometrical, 39
Legend to, 43
Mason's thinking steadily on the meaning of their, 39
purpose of the Masonic, 4, 12
what the candidate learns about the Masonic, 8, 37

T

Tabernacle, the, 34
Taste, 7
definition, 65
See also Senses of the body
Temperance, 11
Temple, 1
not made with hands, 2, 10, 43
second, the, 2, 41
See also King Solomon's Temple
Thinker, the, 13, 15, 26, 43
Boaz, 38
conscious relation with, 37
definition, 66
Fellow Craft, 18, 30, 37, 38
fundamental teachings of Masonry and, 38
Hiram, King of Tyre, 22, 25, 38
Jubelo, 22, 38
pillar of Strength, 38
Second Logos, 36
Senior Warden, 21, 30, 38
the Word and, 35
See also, Reason; Rightness

Thinking, 18, 21
active, 4, 66
definition, 66
masonic, 4
passive, 4, 66
right, 11
thinking that does not create thoughts, that is, destiny, 67
through geometrical symbols, 40
tools of Masonry and, 13, 15, 39
Thought(s), 23
balancing a, 67
balancing factor in a, 67
cable-tow of rebirth and, 21
creation of a, 24
definition, 67
masonic, 4
ruling, 68
symbols and, 39
visiting, 68
Time, 25, 29
definition, 68
is death, 25
Token, the, 10
Tools, the working
Mason, of a, 10, 11, 13, 18
Travels, 7
Trestle-board, 38, 45
designs on the, 11, 21
See also Breath-form
Triangles, 21, 36, 38
Triune Self, the, 7
apron and, 9
columns or pillars and, 14
definition, 68
Intelligent-matter, 16
Jubela, Jubelo, Jebelum, 22
Lights, the great, and, 8
Lodge and, 29
name of, 35
powers, 22, 35
teachings of Masonry and, 37
the Word and, 35
trinity, the, 27
See also Doer, the; Knower, the; Thinker, the
Trust
definition, 68

Truth
  is without color, 40
  symbols and, 40
Truths, great
  locked up in trivial forms, 4
  universal, 17
Twelve, the Great. *See* Zodiac, the
Type(s)
  definition, 68

U

Understanding, 5
  definition, 69
Unit(s)
  definition, 69
  nature, 15, 69
Upright man
  the Mason as an, 9

V

Virtue(s), 11, 37
  definition, 69

W

Wages and jewels, 16
Will, Free, 6
  definition, 69
Wisdom, 26, 38
  definition, 70
Word, the, 11, 13, 22, 32, 34–36, 39
  feeling-and-desire, the doer, 36
  God, of, 8
  Hiram Abiff is, 22
  Lost Word, 22, 36
  meaning of, 35
  pronunciation of, 36
  symbol for, 36
  See also IAOM; Name, the
Work, 4, 7, 30
  definition, 70
Work, the, 15, 19, 31
  contains great truths, 4
  daily, 30
  Entered Apprentice, 7, 14
  Fellow Craft, 14
  inner meanings of, 5

lodge, of the, 29, 30, 32
  Master Mason, 18
  the Great Work, 41
Workmen
  the fifteen, 23
World(s), the
  four, 17
  physical, 17, 35, 40, 46
Worshipful Master. *See* Knower, the;
  Officers

Z

Zodiac, the, 40
  Great Twelve, the, 23
  in the body, 23
  twelve points of, 17, 23, 40
  twelve ultimate beings, 23
  universal truths, 17
  See also Circle, the; Point
    and the Circle, the
Zodiacal signs, the, 17, 45

The Word Foundation

Declaration

The purpose of the Foundation is to make known
the good news in the book Thinking and Destiny
and other writings of the same author, that it is
possible for the conscious self in the human body
to nullify and abolish death by the regeneration and
transformation of the structure of the human into
a perfect and immortal physical body, in which the
self will be consciously immortal.

The Human Being

The conscious self in the human body enters this
world in a hypnotic dream, forgetful of its origin;
it dreams through human life without knowing who
and what it is, awake or asleep; the body dies, and
the self passes out of this world without knowing
how or why it came, or where it goes when it leaves
the body.

Transformation

The good news is, to tell the conscious self in every
human body what it is, how it hypnotized itself by
thinking, and how, by thinking, it can dehypnotize
and know itself as an immortal. In the doing of
this it will change its mortal into a perfect physical
body and, even while in this physical world, it will
be consciously at one with its own Triune Self in the
Realm of Permanence.

Concerning The Word Foundation

This is the time, when the newspapers and books show that crime is rampant; when there continue to be "wars and rumors of wars"; this is the time while the nations are distraught, and death is in the air; yes, this is the time for the establishment of The Word Foundation.

As declared, the purpose of The Word Foundation is for the vanquishing of death by the rebuilding and transformation of the human physical body into a body of immortal life, in which one's conscious self will find itself and return to The Realm of Permanence in The Eternal Order of Progression, which it left in the long, long ago, to enter this man and woman world of time and death.

Not everybody will believe it, not everybody will want it, but everybody should know about it.

This book and other like writings are especially for the few who do want the information and who are willing to pay the price which is in or by the regenerating and transforming of their bodies.

No human being can have conscious immortality after death. Each one must immortalize his or her own physical body to have immortal life; no other inducement is offered; there are no shortcuts or bargains. The only thing that one can do for another is to tell that other that there is the Great Way, as shown in this book. If it does not appeal to the reader he can dismiss the thought of eternal life, and continue to suffer death. But there are some people in this world who are determined to know the truth and to live the life by finding The Way in their own bodies.

Always in this world there have been individuals who disappeared unnoticed, who were determined to reconstruct their human bodies and to find their way to The Realm of Permanence, from which they departed, to come into this man and woman world. Each such one knew that the weight of the world's thought would hinder the work.

By the "world's thought" is meant the mass of people, who ridicule or distrust any innovation for improvement until the method advocated is proven to be true.

But now that it is shown that the great work can be done properly and reasonably, and that others have responded and are engaged in the "Great Work," the world's thought will cease to be a hindrance because The Great Way will be for the good of mankind.

The Word Foundation is for the proving of Conscious Immortality.

H. W. Percival

Other Books

Thinking and Destiny

Many have found *Thinking and Destiny* to be unlike anything they have previously read. The author introduces us to the true meaning and purpose of Man, the Universe and Beyond. Provocative in its vast and detailed subject matter, the information may at first startle, or even elicit skepticism—until its contents have been absorbed. The statements made in this book are not based on speculation, dogma or religious authority. It was Percival's crucial experiences of the Presence of Consciousness as the Ultimate Reality that led to his ability to distill knowledge and truth from a process he called real thinking. Through this system of thinking he was able to provide sound answers to questions that heretofore have been considered by many to be unanswerable; such as, "Where did I come from?" and "Why am I here?" Mr. Percival stated that he was neither preacher nor teacher. He conveyed the information of which he was aware and left it to the individual to decide its veracity for him or herself. *Thinking and Destiny* is a guide for all humanity in a bewildering world. In print for over 65 years, this book is as relevant today as it will be for generations to come because the information is timeless and unaffected by prevalent thought. Reading this book may be one of your most profound and rewarding experiences.

by Harold W. Percival

Man and Woman and Child

This book, simply written, addresses humanity's descent into mortal bodies of birth and death. Here, you will learn the true identity of you—the conscious self in the body—and how you may break the hypnotic spell your senses and thinking have cast about you since childhood. Percival states: "These assertions are not based on fanciful hopes. They are substantiated by the anatomical, physiological, biological and psychological evidences given herein, which you can if you will, examine, consider and judge; and, then do what you think best."

Democracy Is Self-Government

Mr. Percival provides an original concept of "True" Democracy, where personal and national affairs are brought under the spotlight of eternal truths. This is not a political book. It sheds light on the direct connection between the conscious self in every human body and the affairs of the world in which we live. Percival tells us that we each have an opportunity, as well as a duty, to bring eternal Law, Justice, and Harmony to the world. This begins with learning to govern ourselves—our passions, vices, appetites, and behavior. "The purpose of this book is to point the way."—H. W. Percival

To learn more about the Percival books please visit:
theworldfoundation.org